SOU CAROLINA

INSIDEOUT

South Carolina travel guide 2024 & Beyond with essential tourist information, maps, and pictures to make you Explore the city with great confidence

Harper M. Jones

Copyright © 2024 by *Travel Rocket*

All rights reserved.

No part of this book may be reproduced or transmitted in any form or by any means, electronic or mechanical, including photocopying, recording, or by any information storage and retrieval system, without permission in writing from the publisher

Table of Contents

Introduction _____ **6**

Chapter 1: Introduction to South Carolina_____ **10**

    The History and Culture of South Carolina _____ 10

    Geography and Climate of South Carolina _____ 13

    Planning Your Trip to South Carolina _____ 15

Chapter 2: Must-Visit Destinations in South Carolina__ 18

    Charleston: The Historic Gem of South Carolina _____ 18

    Myrtle Beach: Fun in the Sun and Sand _____ 21

    Hilton Head Island: A Paradise for Golfers and Beach Lovers _____ 24

    Columbia: The Capital City with a Rich Heritage _____ 27

    Greenville: Discover the Upstate's Vibrant Art and Food Scene _____ 30

Chapter 3: Outdoor Adventures in South Carolina ____ 34

    Hiking and Camping in the Blue Ridge Mountains _____ 34

    Exploring the Waterfalls and Rivers of South Carolina ___ 37

Kayaking and Canoeing in the Coastal Marshes _____ 40

Fishing and Boating in the Lakes of South Carolina _____ 45

Chapter 4: Historical and Cultural Experiences_____48

Plantation Tours in South Carolina_____ 48

Exploring Gullah Geechee Culture and Heritage _____ 51

Visiting Historic Sites of the Civil War _____ 54

Discovering African American History in South Carolina _ 56

Immersing Yourself in Southern Cuisine and Music _____ 59

Chapter 5: Unique Experiences in South Carolina _____ 62

Swamp Tours and Alligator Spotting _____ 62

Ghost Tours and Haunted Places _____ 64

Discovering the World of Barbecue in South Carolina ___ 67

Exploring the Unique Beaches of South Carolina _____ 70

Festival and Event Highlights in South Carolina _____ 72

Chapter 6: Practical Travel Information _____76

Transportation Options in South Carolina_____ 76

Accommodation Choices for Every Budget _____ 79

Budget Hotels in South Carolina_____ 82

Dining and Local Cuisine Recommendations _____ 110

Safety Tips for Traveling in South Carolina _____ 113

Essential Packing List for Adventurers _____ 116

Chapter7: 6 Day trip from Charleston _____ 120

Visit to Beaufort & the Lowcountry _____ 121

Tour the Ashley River Plantations _____ 123

Stroll a swampy forest at Congaree National Park. _____ 125

Explore the Charleston County Sea Islands _____ 126

Unwind at Brookgreen Gardens _____ 127

Discover the vibrant pulse of Columbia. _____ 128

Chapter 8: Beyond 2025: Future Travel Trends in South Carolina _____ 130

Sustainable Tourism Initiatives in South Carolina _____ 130

Emerging Destinations and Attractions _____ 133

Technological Advancements in Travel Planning _____ 135

Cultural Exchange Programs and Volunteer Opportunities _____ 138

Tips for Responsible Travel in South Carolina _____ 141

Travel Rocket

Recommended Books and Websites for Further Exploration
_____ 144

Useful Contacts and Emergency Numbers_____ 146

Conclusion _____ *150*

EXPLORING
SOUTH CAROLINA
TRAVEL ROCKET

Introduction

Have you ever found yourself in a new city, filled with excitement and anticipation, only to be met with frustration and confusion? Perhaps you wandered aimlessly, unsure of where to go or what to do. You're not alone. Exploring a new destination can be thrilling, but without the right guidance, it can quickly turn into a daunting experience.

Imagine this: You've just arrived in South Carolina, a state rich in history, culture, and natural beauty. The warm Southern hospitality welcomes you, but as you step out into the bustling streets, you're overwhelmed by the sheer magnitude of options. Where do you start? Which attractions are worth visiting? Where can you find the best accommodations, the tastiest food, and the most exciting activities?

Moments like these inspired us to create "South Carolina InsideOut: Your Ultimate Travel Guide 2024 & Beyond." We understand the frustration of navigating a new city without a proper guide. That's why we've meticulously curated this comprehensive travel companion to ensure that your journey through South Carolina is nothing short of extraordinary.

Within the pages of this guide, you'll find essential tourist information, detailed maps, and captivating pictures to empower you to explore the city with confidence. Say goodbye to aimless wandering and hello to unforgettable adventures. Whether you're a history buff, a nature enthusiast, a foodie, or an adrenaline junkie, we've got you covered.

Discover the fascinating history of South Carolina, from its colonial roots to its pivotal role in shaping American history. Find the perfect accommodation to suit your budget and preferences, whether you prefer luxurious resorts or cozy budget hotels. Navigate the city with ease using our comprehensive transportation guide. Uncover the top attractions, insider tips, and hidden gems that only the locals know about.

Immerse yourself in the vibrant culture of South Carolina by attending local festivals, exploring world-class museums, and indulging in the art of Southern hospitality. Shop till you drop in charming neighborhoods filled with unique boutiques and artisanal shops. Embark on thrilling adventures, from kayaking through scenic waterways to hiking in pristine natural parks.

Rest assured, we've got you covered in case of emergencies, with essential contact information readily available at your fingertips.

So, are you ready to embark on the ultimate South Carolina adventure? Let "South Carolina InsideOut" be your trusted companion as you journey through the Palmetto State and beyond. Say goodbye to frustration and hello to unforgettable memories. Your South Carolina adventure starts here.

Chapter 1: Introduction to South Carolina

The History and Culture of South Carolina

South Carolina, a state rich in history and culture, offers an unforgettable adventure for tourists, adventurers, travelers, and explorers alike. From its captivating past to its vibrant present, this subchapter will take you on a journey through time, unveiling the essence of South Carolina.

Step back in time and discover the roots of South Carolina's history. The state played a significant role in the American Revolution and was the first to declare independence from British rule. Visit historic sites such as Fort Sumter, where the first shots of the Civil War were fired, and immerse yourself in the stories that shaped the nation.

South Carolina's culture is deeply rooted in its African, European, and Native American heritage. Experience the Gullah Geechee culture, a unique blend of West African traditions and English influences, by visiting the Sea Islands. Explore the rich heritage of the Cherokee Nation at the Oconaluftee Indian Village or witness the vibrant European influence in Charleston's historic architecture.

For those seeking outdoor adventures, South Carolina offers a myriad of opportunities. Embark on an unforgettable hike through the awe-inspiring landscapes of the Blue Ridge Mountains or explore the lush swamps of Congaree National Park, home to an abundance of wildlife. The state's pristine coastline beckons with miles of sandy beaches, perfect for swimming, sunbathing, and water sports.

No visit to South Carolina is complete without indulging in its renowned culinary delights. Sample the authentic flavors of low-country cuisine, featuring fresh seafood, rice, and flavorful spices. From shrimp and grits to she-crab soup, your taste buds will be tantalized by the unique blend of flavors that define the region.

Immerse yourself in the vibrant festivals and events that celebrate South Carolina's culture. From the world-famous Spoleto Festival USA in Charleston, showcasing a diverse range of performing arts, to the Beaufort Water Festival, where you can experience traditional Southern hospitality, there is always something to celebrate in South Carolina.

As you delve into the history and culture of South Carolina, you will be captivated by its fascinating past and dynamic present. Whether you are a history enthusiast, nature lover, or simply seeking a memorable adventure, South Carolina promises to be the ultimate destination for your travel aspirations in 2024-2025 and beyond.

So, pack your bags, embark on this ultimate adventure travel guide, and let South Carolina mesmerize you with its rich history, vibrant culture, and boundless possibilities.

Geography and Climate of South Carolina

South Carolina, located in the southeastern region of the United States, offers a myriad of natural wonders and diverse landscapes that will captivate the hearts of any tourist, adventurer, traveler, or explorer. With its stunning coastline, rolling hills, and lush forests, the state is a true paradise for outdoor enthusiasts seeking unforgettable experiences.

The geography of South Carolina is incredibly diverse, offering a unique blend of coastal plains, the majestic Blue Ridge Mountains, and everything in between. The state is bordered by the Atlantic Ocean to the east, boasting over 200 miles of pristine shoreline. From the bustling beaches of Myrtle Beach to the secluded islands of the Lowcountry, South Carolina's coast is a haven for sun-seekers, water sports enthusiasts, and nature lovers alike.

Venturing inland, visitors will encounter the picturesque Piedmont region, characterized by gently sloping hills and fertile farmland. This area is home to charming small towns, historic sites, and sprawling plantations, providing a glimpse into the state's rich cultural heritage.

To the west lies the awe-inspiring Blue Ridge Mountains, part of the larger Appalachian Mountain range. Here, adventurers can explore stunning national parks, such as the Great Smoky Mountains, where hiking, camping, and wildlife-spotting opportunities abound. The Blue Ridge Mountains also offer breathtaking scenic drives, including the famous Blue Ridge Parkway, showcasing panoramic vistas and vibrant fall foliage.

South Carolina's climate is generally mild and welcoming, with hot summers and mild winters. The coastal areas enjoy a subtropical climate, while the inland regions experience a more continental climate. This diversity of climates makes South Carolina a year-round destination, offering something for every season.

The state's natural beauty is further enhanced by its abundant wildlife and biodiversity. Nature enthusiasts can spot a wide variety of species, including alligators, dolphins, sea turtles, and the elusive red wolf, to name just a few. South Carolina's numerous state parks and protected areas provide ample opportunities for hiking, birdwatching, kayaking, and other outdoor activities.

Whether you seek the thrill of surfing the Atlantic waves, embarking on a scenic mountain hike, or immersing yourself in the rich history and culture of South Carolina's towns, this ultimate adventure travel guide for 2024-2025 and beyond will be your trusted companion in exploring all the wonders this magnificent state has to offer.

Planning Your Trip to South Carolina

South Carolina, the ultimate adventure travel destination, beckons tourists, adventurers, travelers, and explorers from around the world. With its stunning coastline, charming historic towns, lush forests, and vibrant cities, this southeastern state promises an unforgettable experience. To help you make the most of your visit, this subchapter provides a comprehensive guide to planning your trip to South Carolina.

First, decide on your preferred time to visit. South Carolina enjoys a mild climate year-round, but each season offers unique experiences. Spring brings blooming flowers and ideal temperatures, while summer is perfect for beachgoers and water sports enthusiasts. Fall showcases the state's stunning foliage, and winter offers a quieter, more serene atmosphere.

Next, determine your interests and the areas of South Carolina you'd like to explore. Are you drawn to the coastal beauty and historic charm of Charleston? Or perhaps you're seeking outdoor adventures in the Upstate region, with its picturesque mountains and waterfalls? Consider the distinct regions of South Carolina and the activities that appeal to you the most.

Once you've identified your preferred destinations, it's time to plan your itinerary. Start by researching the attractions, landmarks, and activities available in each area. From exploring the historic plantations of Charleston to hiking the breathtaking trails of the Blue Ridge Mountains, South Carolina offers a wealth of experiences for every taste.

Don't forget to delve into the local cuisine. South Carolina is renowned for its delicious culinary offerings, including mouth-watering barbecue, fresh seafood, and signature dishes like shrimp and grits. Explore the diverse dining options and make a list of must-try dishes to savor during your trip.

Accommodation is another crucial aspect of trip planning. South Carolina boasts a range of accommodations, from luxurious beachfront resorts to cozy bed and breakfasts in historic towns. Research and book your lodging well in advance to secure the best deals and ensure availability during peak seasons.

Lastly, consider transportation options. South Carolina is well-served by major airports, making it easily accessible for international travelers. Renting a car is recommended for exploring the state at your own pace, but public transportation, such as buses and trains, can also be utilized.

By following these steps, you'll be well-prepared to embark on an incredible adventure through the diverse landscapes and rich culture of South Carolina. From the tranquil beaches to the vibrant cities, this subchapter serves as your guide to planning a memorable trip to South Carolina in 2024-2025 and beyond. Get ready to create lifelong memories and immerse yourself in the charm of the Palmetto State.

Chapter 2: Must-Visit Destinations in South Carolina

Charleston: The Historic Gem of South Carolina

Welcome to Charleston, the historic gem of South Carolina! Nestled along the coast, this charming city boasts a rich history, breathtaking architecture, and a vibrant culture that will captivate tourists, adventurers, travelers, and explorers alike. Whether you're seeking an immersive historical experience, a culinary adventure, or a leisurely stroll through picturesque streets, Charleston has it all.

History comes alive in Charleston, where every cobblestone and grand mansion has a story to tell. Begin your exploration at the iconic Battery, a promenade overlooking Charleston Harbor, where you can marvel at the stunning views and learn about the city's maritime past. Don't miss a visit to Fort Sumter, the site where the first shots of the Civil War were fired, offering a fascinating glimpse into our nation's history.

As you wander through the streets of Charleston, be prepared to be whisked away to another era. The historic district is a treasure trove of beautifully preserved homes, gardens, and churches, showcasing architectural styles ranging from Georgian to Greek Revival. Take a guided walking tour to uncover hidden gems and hear captivating tales of the city's past. And if you're a lover of all things spooky, make sure to explore the haunted side of Charleston on a ghost tour - an eerie adventure you won't soon forget.

No visit to Charleston would be complete without indulging in its culinary delights. The city has gained a reputation as a food lover's paradise, with a diverse array of restaurants offering everything from traditional Southern cuisine to innovative farm-to-table creations. Sample mouth-watering shrimp and grits, enjoy a Lowcountry boil, or savor some of the best barbecues in the South. Don't forget to finish off your meal with a classic Charleston dessert - the delectable pecan pie.

For those seeking outdoor adventures, Charleston's natural beauty will not disappoint. Explore the neighboring barrier islands, such as Sullivan's Island and Isle of Palms, where pristine beaches and abundant wildlife await. Embark on a kayaking expedition through the salt marshes, or set sail for a sunset cruise along the coast. And if you're a golfer, tee off at one of the world-class golf courses that dot the area.

Charleston truly offers an unforgettable experience for travelers, adventurers, and explorers. As you immerse yourself in its history, savor its cuisine, and bask in its natural beauty, you'll come to understand why this city is a must-visit destination in South Carolina and beyond. So pack your bags, embark on an ultimate adventure, and prepare to fall in love with the historic gem that is Charleston.

Myrtle Beach: Fun in the Sun and Sand

Welcome to Myrtle Beach, the ultimate destination for fun, relaxation, and adventure! Nestled along the beautiful South Carolina coastline, this vibrant city offers something for every traveler seeking an unforgettable experience. Whether you're a tourist, adventurer, traveler, or explorer, Myrtle Beach is the perfect place to immerse yourself in the natural beauty and rich culture of South Carolina.

As you step onto the sandy shores of Myrtle Beach, you'll be greeted by miles of pristine coastline and crystal-clear waters. This subchapter of "Exploring South Carolina: The Ultimate Adventure Travel Guide 2024-2025" is dedicated to unveiling the myriad of activities and attractions that await you in this beachfront paradise.

For those seeking an adrenaline rush, Myrtle Beach offers a plethora of thrilling water sports, such as jet skiing, parasailing, and paddleboarding. Ride the waves, feel the ocean breeze on your face, and create lasting memories of your adventure-filled vacation.

If relaxation is more your style, grab a beach chair or towel and soak up the sun while listening to the soothing sound of crashing waves. Myrtle Beach boasts over 60 miles of uninterrupted coastline, providing ample space for sunbathing, beachcombing, and building sandcastles with your loved ones.

Beyond the beach, Myrtle Beach is home to a myriad of attractions that cater to all interests and ages. Explore the iconic Myrtle Beach Boardwalk, famous for its lively atmosphere, thrilling rides, and mouth-watering cuisine. Indulge in fresh seafood, enjoy live music, and browse through unique shops offering local crafts and souvenirs.

For nature enthusiasts, venture a short distance from the bustling city center to discover the breathtaking beauty of Myrtle Beach State Park. This pristine coastal preserve offers hiking trails, camping grounds, and a picturesque fishing pier, allowing you to reconnect with nature and experience South Carolina's diverse wildlife.

As the sun sets over Myrtle Beach, the city transforms into a vibrant hub of entertainment. From live theaters showcasing Broadway-quality shows to lively nightclubs and bars, there's never a dull moment. Catch a captivating performance, dance the night away, or simply enjoy a romantic stroll along the boardwalk under the starlit sky.

Myrtle Beach truly is a destination that promises unlimited fun, adventure, and relaxation. So pack your bags, embark on this ultimate adventure, and let the sun and sand of Myrtle Beach create memories that will last a lifetime.

Join us in exploring South Carolina's coastal gem and uncover the wonders that await you in Myrtle Beach.

Hilton Head Island: A Paradise for Golfers and Beach Lovers

Welcome to Hilton Head Island, a true paradise for both golfers and beach lovers. Situated in the beautiful state of South Carolina, this enchanting island offers a unique blend of natural beauty, outdoor adventure, and world-class golfing experiences that will leave you in awe.

For avid golfers, Hilton Head Island boasts over 20 championship golf courses, making it a golfer's dream destination. Designed by legendary architects such as Pete Dye, Jack Nicklaus, and Robert Trent Jones, these courses offer a variety of challenges and stunning views that will captivate players of all skill levels. Whether you're a beginner or a seasoned pro, you'll find a course that suits your style and provides an unforgettable golfing experience.

But Hilton Head Island offers much more than just golf. With its 12 miles of pristine beaches, this island paradise is a haven for beach lovers. From sunbathing and swimming to building sandcastles and beachcombing, there are endless opportunities to relax and soak up the sun on Hilton Head's sandy shores. For the more adventurous souls, the island offers a range of water sports, including kayaking, paddleboarding, and parasailing, allowing you to explore crystal-clear waters and get your adrenaline pumping.

Beyond the golf courses and beaches, Hilton Head Island is also home to a vibrant culinary scene, with numerous restaurants offering delicious seafood and Lowcountry specialties. Indulge in fresh shrimp, oysters, and crab dishes, or savor the unique flavors of Gullah cuisine, a traditional African-American cooking style that has deep roots in the region.

For nature enthusiasts, Hilton Head Island provides ample opportunities to explore its diverse ecosystem. Take a leisurely bike ride along the island's many trails, where you'll encounter stunning wildlife, including dolphins, alligators, and a variety of bird species. You can also visit the Pinckney Island National Wildlife Refuge, a protected area that offers hiking trails and birdwatching opportunities.

As you plan your visit to Hilton Head Island, be sure to check out the annual events and festivals that take place throughout the year, such as the RBC Heritage Golf Tournament and the Hilton Head Island Wine and Food Festival. These events showcase the island's rich culture, community spirit, and love for all things golf and beach-related.

So, whether you're a golf enthusiast, a beach lover, or simply an adventurer seeking new experiences, Hilton Head Island is the perfect destination for your next escape. With its stunning landscapes, world-class golf courses, pristine beaches, and vibrant culture, this island paradise is sure to leave an indelible mark on your travel memories. Come and explore Hilton Head Island and discover why it truly is a golfer's and beach lover's paradise.

Columbia: The Capital City with a Rich Heritage

When it comes to exploring the beautiful state of South Carolina, no trip would be complete without a visit to its capital city, Columbia. Nestled in the heart of the state, this vibrant city is not only the political hub but also a cultural and historical treasure trove. With its diverse attractions and rich heritage, Columbia promises an unforgettable experience for tourists, adventurers, travelers, and explorers alike.

Columbia boasts a range of attractions that cater to all interests and preferences. For history enthusiasts, the city offers a fascinating journey back in time. Start your exploration at the South Carolina State House, an iconic landmark that showcases stunning architecture and significant political history. Take a guided tour to learn about the state's governance and admire the breathtaking dome. Just a short walk away, you'll discover the South Carolina State Museum, where you can delve into the state's past through interactive exhibits and engaging displays.

To further understand Columbia's history, a visit to the Historic Columbia Foundation is a must.

This organization preserves and showcases the city's historic homes and gardens, transporting visitors to a bygone era. Explore the Robert Mills House, a National Historic Landmark, or stroll through the enchanting gardens at the Hampton-Preston Mansion. Immerse yourself in the stories of the past and gain a deeper appreciation for Columbia's heritage.

Beyond its historical significance, Columbia also offers a vibrant arts and cultural scene. The Columbia Museum of Art presents an impressive collection of European, American, and Asian art, as well as rotating exhibits that showcase local talent.

If you're a music lover, catch a performance at the Koger Center for the Arts or the Township Auditorium, both renowned venues that host a variety of shows throughout the year.

Nature enthusiasts will also find solace in Columbia's abundant green spaces. The Riverbanks Zoo and Garden is a world-class facility that houses a diverse range of animals and provides a picturesque setting for a leisurely stroll. For those seeking outdoor adventure, the Congaree National Park is a short drive away, offering hiking trails through ancient forests and the opportunity to kayak or canoe along the Congaree River.

As you explore Columbia, be sure to indulge in its culinary delights. The city boasts a thriving food scene that reflects its rich cultural diversity. From Southern comfort food to international cuisine, there's something to satisfy every palate. Don't forget to try some classic South Carolina barbecue and sample the local delicacies.

Columbia stands as a captivating destination within the vibrant state of South Carolina. With its historical significance, cultural offerings, and natural beauty, this capital city promises an unforgettable adventure for all who visit. So, whether you're a history buff, an art enthusiast, or an outdoor adventurer, Columbia should be at the top of your travel list when exploring South Carolina in 2024-2025 and beyond.

Greenville: Discover the Upstate's Vibrant Art and Food Scene

Welcome to Greenville, South Carolina, a hidden gem nestled in the heart of the Upstate region. Known for its vibrant art and food scene, this city offers a unique blend of southern charm, natural beauty, and cultural experiences that are sure to captivate tourists, adventurers, travelers, and explorers alike.

Art enthusiasts will delight in Greenville's thriving art community. The city boasts a host of galleries, museums, and public art installations that showcase the work of both local and internationally renowned artists. Take a stroll through the downtown area and be enchanted by the vibrant murals that adorn the walls, or visit the Greenville County Museum of Art to admire its impressive collection of American art. For a more immersive experience, catch a performance at the Peace Center for the Performing Arts, where you can enjoy everything from Broadway shows to symphony concerts.

No visit to Greenville is complete without indulging in its delectable food scene. The city has gained a reputation as a culinary hotspot, offering an array of dining options that cater to all tastes and budgets. From farm-to-table restaurants that serve up fresh, locally sourced ingredients to international eateries that showcase flavors from around the globe, Greenville is a food lover's paradise. Don't forget to sample some traditional southern dishes, such as fried chicken and shrimp and grits, at one of the city's many soul food joints.

Beyond its art and food offerings, Greenville also boasts stunning natural beauty. The city is surrounded by picturesque landscapes, including the breathtaking Blue Ridge Mountains and the scenic Falls Park on the Reedy.

Take a hike along the Swamp Rabbit Trail, a 22-mile greenway that winds through the city and offers stunning views of the surrounding countryside. Or, for a more leisurely experience, enjoy a picnic in one of the city's many parks or explore the charming shops and cafes along Main Street.

Whether you're seeking cultural experiences, culinary delights, or outdoor adventures, Greenville has something to offer every traveler.

Plan your visit to this vibrant city and discover why it has quickly become one of South Carolina's top destinations. With its rich arts scene, diverse culinary offerings, and stunning natural beauty, Greenville is sure to leave a lasting impression on adventurers, travelers, and explorers for years to come.

Chapter 3: Outdoor Adventures in South Carolina

Hiking and Camping in the Blue Ridge Mountains

As you embark on your adventure in South Carolina, prepare to be captivated by the awe-inspiring beauty of the Blue Ridge Mountains. Nestled in the western part of the state, this majestic range offers an abundance of exciting opportunities for hiking and camping enthusiasts. Get ready to explore nature at its finest and create unforgettable memories in the heart of the wilderness.

South Carolina's Blue Ridge Mountains boast a diverse range of trails catering to all skill levels, making it the perfect destination for both seasoned hikers and beginners alike. Lace-up your boots and choose from a myriad of paths that wind through lush forests, meander alongside babbling brooks, and lead to breathtaking vistas. Whether you prefer a leisurely stroll or a challenging uphill climb, there is a trail waiting to fulfill your every desire.

For those seeking a true wilderness experience, camping in the Blue Ridge Mountains is an absolute must. Pitch your tent in one of the many scenic campgrounds and fall asleep under a canopy of stars serenaded by the soothing sounds of nature. Wake up to the crisp mountain air and embark on a day filled with exploration and adventure.

In addition to its natural beauty, the Blue Ridge Mountains also offer a range of outdoor activities to satisfy the thrill-seekers among us. Test your skills on exhilarating rock climbing routes, feel the rush of adrenaline as you navigate white-water rapids, or embark on a mountain biking expedition through rugged terrain. The possibilities are endless, and the sense of accomplishment and fulfillment that come with conquering these challenges is truly unparalleled.

As you venture into the wilderness, it is important to remember to respect and preserve the natural environment. Leave no trace behind, stay on designated trails, and abide by all camping regulations to ensure future generations can enjoy the same pristine beauty that you have encountered.

So, whether you are a tourist looking to explore the hidden gems of South Carolina or an adventurer seeking an adrenaline rush, the Blue Ridge Mountains offer a playground of natural wonders waiting to be discovered. Grab your backpack, lace up your boots, and immerse yourself in the beauty and tranquility of this breathtaking mountain range. Your ultimate adventure awaits in the Blue Ridge Mountains of South Carolina.

Exploring the Waterfalls and Rivers of South Carolina

Welcome to South Carolina, a state full of natural wonders waiting to be discovered! In this subchapter, we will take you on an adventure through the breathtaking waterfalls and majestic rivers that flow through this beautiful southern state. Whether you are a tourist, adventurer, traveler, or explorer, get ready to witness the unparalleled beauty that South Carolina has to offer.

South Carolina is home to an impressive array of waterfalls, each with its own unique charm. One of the most iconic waterfalls is White-water Falls, located in the scenic Jocassee Gorges. As the highest waterfall east of the Rocky Mountains, White-water Falls cascades down a staggering 411 feet, creating a mesmerizing sight that will leave you in awe.

For those seeking a more off-the-beaten-path experience, a visit to Raven Cliff Falls is a must. Nestled in Caesars Head State Park, this captivating waterfall plunges 420 feet down a sheer rock face, surrounded by lush greenery and tranquil hiking trails. The hike to the falls is an adventure in itself, offering panoramic views of the surrounding mountains and forests.

But the beauty of South Carolina doesn't end with its waterfalls. The state is also blessed with a network of picturesque rivers, perfect for kayaking, canoeing, and fishing. The Congaree River, winding through Congaree National Park, provides a serene escape into nature. Paddle along its gentle currents, surrounded by towering cypress trees and abundant wildlife, and immerse yourself in the tranquility of the great outdoors.

If you're seeking a more adventurous river experience, look no further than the Chattooga River. As a designated Wild and Scenic River, it offers exhilarating white-water rafting opportunities for thrill-seekers. Challenge yourself with Class IV rapids and navigate through stunning river gorges, all while taking in the breathtaking beauty of the surrounding wilderness.

As you explore the waterfalls and rivers of South Carolina, make sure to also indulge in the vibrant culture and rich history that the state has to offer. From charming small towns to bustling cities, there is something for everyone in this diverse and captivating destination.

So pack your bags, grab your camera, and embark on an unforgettable adventure through the waterfalls and rivers of South Carolina. Get ready to create lifelong memories and discover the hidden gems of this enchanting state. South Carolina Travel Guide 2024-2025 and beyond is your ultimate companion in exploring the wonders that await you in this remarkable corner of the United States.

Kayaking and Canoeing in the Coastal Marshes

Welcome to the enchanting coastal marshes of South Carolina, where adventure awaits! If you're a fan of outdoor exploration, kayaking and canoeing in these stunning marshlands is an experience like no other. Get ready to immerse yourself in the beauty of nature, discover hidden gems, and create memories that will last a lifetime.

Why choose kayaking or canoeing in the coastal marshes? Well, first and foremost, it's an excellent way to connect with the unique ecosystem that thrives here. As you paddle through the calm waters, you'll be surrounded by lush greenery, abundant wildlife, and breathtaking landscapes. The marshes are home to a variety of bird species, including herons, egrets, and ospreys, so keep your eyes peeled for these magnificent creatures as you navigate through the waterways.

Whether you're a seasoned kayaker or a beginner, there are options for everyone. Local outfitters offer guided tours that cater to different skill levels, ensuring a safe and enjoyable experience for all. These knowledgeable guides will lead you to the most picturesque spots, share fascinating stories about the area's history, and provide interesting insights into the marshland's delicate ecosystem.

For the more adventurous souls, consider embarking on a multi-day kayaking or canoeing expedition. Imagine camping under a canopy of stars, waking up to the gentle sounds of nature, and exploring remote corners of the marshes that are inaccessible by foot. These extended trips offer a deeper connection with the environment and an opportunity to truly disconnect from the modern world.

No matter the duration of your kayak or canoe adventure, be prepared to be mesmerized by the serenity and tranquility of the marshes. The slow pace of paddling allows you to fully appreciate the beauty around you and provides a sense of calm that is often hard to find in our fast-paced lives.

So, grab your paddle, put on your sunscreen, and get ready to embark on an unforgettable expedition through the coastal marshes of South Carolina. Whether you're a nature lover, adventure seeker, or simply looking to escape the ordinary, kayaking and canoeing in these marshlands will leave you in awe of the wonders that Mother Nature has to offer.

Wildlife Watching in the Francis Marion National Forest

Nestled in the heart of South Carolina, the Francis Marion National Forest is a hidden gem for wildlife enthusiasts, offering an unparalleled opportunity to observe and connect with the region's diverse ecosystem. Whether you are a tourist, adventurer, traveler, or explorer, this vast wilderness promises an unforgettable experience that will truly immerse you in the beauty of nature.

Spanning over 250,000 acres, the Francis Marion National Forest is a haven for wildlife, boasting an incredible array of species. As you traverse its meandering trails, keep your eyes peeled for the majestic white-tailed deer gracefully leaping through the forest or the elusive red fox blending seamlessly with its surroundings. If you're lucky, you may even catch a glimpse of the endangered red-cockaded woodpecker diligently tapping away at the towering longleaf pine trees.

Birdwatchers will be in awe as they encounter a multitude of avian species that call this forest home. From the vibrant warblers darting through the foliage to the regal bald eagles soaring overhead, every turn in the trail presents an opportunity to witness the wonders of South Carolina's feathered inhabitants. Don't forget to bring your binoculars and camera to capture these remarkable moments.

For those seeking a more aquatic adventure, the Francis Marion National Forest offers prime opportunities for kayaking and canoeing along its tranquil blackwater rivers and serene cypress swamps. As you navigate through these pristine waterways, keep an eye out for the American alligator basking on the banks or the playful river otters frolicking in the cool waters. Exploring these unique habitats will provide an up-close and personal encounter with the incredible biodiversity of this region.

To make the most of your wildlife-watching experience, consider joining a guided tour led by knowledgeable naturalists who can provide valuable insights into the forest's flora and fauna. These experts will share their wealth of knowledge about the behaviors and habitats of various species, enhancing your understanding and appreciation of the intricate web of life that exists within the Francis Marion National Forest.

So, whether you're a nature enthusiast, an avid photographer, or simply someone seeking a peaceful escape into the wilderness, the Francis Marion National Forest is a must-visit destination in South Carolina. With its abundant wildlife and breathtaking landscapes, this forest promises an adventure like no other. Immerse yourself in the beauty of nature and create memories that will last a lifetime in this remarkable wilderness.

Fishing and Boating in the Lakes of South Carolina

South Carolina, the Palmetto State, is not only famous for its historic landmarks and beautiful beaches but also for its stunning lakes that offer a paradise for fishing and boating enthusiasts. Whether you are a tourist, adventurer, traveler, or explorer, the lakes in South Carolina are a must-visit destination for an unforgettable experience.

Lake Marion, the largest lake in South Carolina, spans over 110,000 acres and is a haven for anglers. Known for its abundant wildlife and vast fishing opportunities, this lake is home to various species, including largemouth bass, catfish, crappie, and striped bass. The lake's calm waters and scenic surroundings make it an ideal spot for boating as well. Rent a boat, sail across the lake, and immerse yourself in the tranquility of nature.

Lake Moultrie, connected to Lake Marion through a canal, is another gem for fishing enthusiasts. Spanning over 60,000 acres, this lake is teeming with largemouth bass, bream, catfish, and crappie. For those seeking an adrenaline rush, Lake Moultrie also offers thrilling opportunities for water sports, such as jet skiing and wakeboarding. Rent a jet ski and feel the wind rushing through your hair as you glide across the lake's sparkling waters.

Lake Jocassee, nestled in the picturesque Blue Ridge Mountains, is a hidden treasure for explorers seeking a unique fishing experience. Known for its crystal-clear waters, this lake is home to various species, including trout, bass, and catfish. Take a peaceful fishing trip, surrounded by breathtaking mountain views, and let the tranquility of the lake wash away your worries.

Lake Murray, a 50,000-acre reservoir, is not only a popular fishing destination but also a hub for boating enthusiasts. With its numerous marinas and boat rental services, you can easily embark on a boating adventure and explore the lake's numerous coves and islands. Don't forget to bring your fishing gear along, as Lake Murray is known for its abundant population of striped bass, catfish, and crappie.

In addition to the breathtaking lakes, South Carolina also offers numerous fishing and boating tournaments throughout the year. Immerse yourself in the local fishing culture by participating in these events or simply enjoy watching skilled anglers showcase their expertise.

Whether you are an experienced angler or a novice adventurer, the lakes of South Carolina offer an unforgettable experience for all. Plan your visit to these stunning lakes and indulge in the thrill of fishing or the serenity of boating. Let South Carolina's natural beauty be the backdrop to your ultimate adventure in 2024-2025 and beyond.

Chapter 4: Historical and Cultural Experiences

Plantation Tours in South Carolina

South Carolina is a state steeped in history and charm, with its picturesque plantations serving as a window into the past. For tourists, adventurers, travelers, and explorers seeking a unique and immersive experience, plantation tours in South Carolina offer a captivating journey back in time. In this subchapter, we will delve into the fascinating world of plantation tours, exploring the rich heritage, architectural marvels, and captivating stories that await visitors.

Embarking on a plantation tour in South Carolina is like stepping into a time capsule. These meticulously preserved estates transport visitors to the antebellum era, showcasing the grandeur and legacy of the Old South. Magnolia Plantation, for instance, is a must-visit destination. With its stunning gardens, scenic marsh views, and a plantation house that dates back to the early 18th century, it offers an enchanting glimpse into plantation life.

Another gem is Boone Hall Plantation, one of America's oldest working plantations. Its iconic Avenue of Oaks, lined with majestic live oak trees, creates an awe-inspiring entrance. Visitors can explore the plantation's rich history, take guided tours of the mansion, and even experience the Gullah culture through interactive exhibits.

Middleton Place, a National Historic Landmark, is renowned for its breathtaking gardens, meticulously landscaped in the 18th-century style. Meandering through its pathways, visitors can marvel at the camellias, azaleas, and other native flora while also exploring the plantation house and the stable yards.

For a deeper understanding of the African American experience on plantations, the McLeod Plantation Historic Site offers a thought-provoking journey. This site sheds light on the lives of enslaved individuals and their contributions to the Lowcountry's history. Guided tours, exhibits, and interactive displays present a more comprehensive narrative of the plantation era.

Beyond the grandeur of the plantations themselves, visitors can also engage in various activities and events. From carriage rides and nature walks to culinary experiences and seasonal festivals, there is something for everyone. Many plantations also offer educational programs, making them ideal for families and history enthusiasts alike.

Plantation tours in South Carolina offer an unforgettable adventure, immersing visitors in the rich history and captivating stories of the Old South. Whether exploring the stunning gardens, delving into the lives of enslaved individuals, or simply marveling at the architectural wonders, these tours provide a unique opportunity to connect with the past. So, embark on this ultimate adventure and let South Carolina's plantations be your gateway to a bygone era.

Exploring Gullah Geechee Culture and Heritage

Immerse yourself in the rich tapestry of South Carolina's Gullah Geechee culture and heritage, an experience that will transport you back in time and leave an indelible mark on your heart. This subchapter of "Exploring South Carolina: The Ultimate Adventure Travel Guide 2024-2025" invites you to embark on a journey unlike any other, delving into the vibrant history and unique traditions of the Gullah Geechee people.

Venturing into the heart of the Lowcountry, you will encounter a captivating culture that has stood the test of time. The Gullah Geechee, descendants of West African slaves, have preserved their African language, customs, and beliefs, creating a distinct and awe-inspiring way of life that is celebrated to this day.

Your exploration begins with a visit to the historic town of Beaufort, where the Gullah Geechee Heritage Corridor reveals the remarkable story of these resilient people. Here, you can engage with local community members who are passionate about sharing their heritage, offering insightful tours and interactive experiences that will deepen your understanding of Gullah Geechee culture.

Immerse yourself in the rhythmic beats of Gullah Geechee music, a soul-stirring fusion of African, European, and Caribbean influences. Attend a lively performance or even learn to play traditional instruments like the gourd banjo or the hand drum, connecting with the vibrant sounds that have echoed through generations.

As you wander through the charming coastal villages of St. Helena Island and Daufuskie Island, you will encounter the traditional crafts that have become synonymous with Gullah Geechee culture. Admire the intricate sweetgrass baskets, handwoven with love and care, and learn about their historical significance from the skilled artisans who create them.

To truly appreciate the essence of Gullah Geechee cuisine, indulge in a culinary adventure that will tantalize your taste buds. Sample dishes like shrimp and grits, okra gumbo, and Hoppin' John are all prepared with the freshest local ingredients and infused with the flavors of the African diaspora. Engage in a cooking class or savor these delectable creations at local restaurants that specialize in Gullah Geechee cuisine.

No exploration of Gullah Geechee culture would be complete without attending a heritage festival or event. Witness the exuberant celebrations of Juneteenth, Emancipation Day, or the Penn Center's Heritage Days, where music, dance, storytelling, and traditional crafts come together to showcase the vibrancy of this remarkable culture.

As you bid farewell to the Gullah Geechee region, you will carry with you a deep appreciation for the strength, resilience, and creativity of people who have shaped the very fabric of South Carolina. This subchapter offers a glimpse into a world that is both enchanting and enlightening, inviting you to embark on a journey of discovery that will forever be etched in your memory.

Visiting Historic Sites of the Civil War

South Carolina, known for its rich history and deep roots in the American Civil War, offers a unique experience for tourists, adventurers, travelers, and explorers seeking to delve into the past. Exploring the historic sites of the Civil War in this state is an ultimate adventure that should not be missed.

From the moment you step foot in South Carolina, you are transported back in time. The remnants of battlefields, historic homes, and memorials stand as a testament to the sacrifices made during this tumultuous period. As you embark on your journey, prepare to be captivated by the stories that unfold before your eyes.

One of the must-visit destinations for any history enthusiast is Fort Sumter National Monument. Located in Charleston, this iconic fort holds immense significance as the site where the first shots of the Civil War were fired. Take a guided tour and learn about the events that led to the conflict and the enduring impact it had on the nation.

Another noteworthy stop is the South Carolina State House in Columbia. This architectural masterpiece not only serves as the seat of government but also holds historical artifacts and exhibits that shed light on the state's role in the Civil War. Walk in the footsteps of the past and discover the intricate details of South Carolina's involvement in this defining moment.

For a deeper understanding of the war's impact on the lives of soldiers and civilians, head to the South Carolina Confederate Relic Room and Military Museum in Columbia. Explore the extensive collection of artifacts, weaponry, and personal mementos that provide a glimpse into the harsh realities of the time.

A visit to the historic town of Beaufort is also a must for history enthusiasts. Here, you can explore the Penn Center, one of the first schools for freed slaves, and gain insight into the struggles and triumphs of African Americans during the Civil War era. Immerse yourself in the rich cultural heritage that has withstood the test of time.

From the rolling hills of Upstate South Carolina to the charming coastal towns, the state's historic sites of the Civil

War offer an adventure that transports you back to a pivotal moment in American history. As you explore these destinations, embrace the opportunity to learn, reflect, and appreciate the sacrifices made by those who came before us. South Carolina's past is waiting to be discovered, and it will leave an indelible mark on your journey.

Discovering African American History in South Carolina

South Carolina, often referred to as the "cradle of the Civil Rights Movement," holds a rich and fascinating history that reflects the struggles, triumphs, and contributions of African Americans. As you embark on your journey through the beautiful state of South Carolina, make sure to explore its African American history to truly understand its cultural significance and profound impact on American society.

One of the most important sites to visit is the Avery Research Center for African American History and Culture in Charleston. This center is dedicated to preserving and promoting the history and culture of African Americans in South Carolina and beyond. Through its exhibits, lectures, and events, visitors can gain a deeper understanding of the

African American experience in the state and its influence on the wider American narrative.

Another must-visit destination is the Penn Center on St. Helena Island. Established in 1862, this historic site served as one of the first schools for freed slaves and played a pivotal role in educating and empowering African Americans during the Reconstruction era. Today, the Penn Center continues to honor its legacy by offering educational programs, cultural events, and exhibits that shed light on the contributions of African Americans to the state's history.

For a truly immersive experience, head to Gullah Geechee Corridor, a stretch of coastline that spans from North Carolina to Florida. This region is home to the Gullah Geechee people, descendants of West African slaves who have preserved their unique language, traditions, and culture for generations. Exploring the Gullah Geechee Corridor allows you to witness the living history of African Americans in South Carolina and gain insight into their vibrant heritage.

In addition to these specific destinations, many cities and towns throughout South Carolina boast significant African

American historical sites. From the Old Slave Mart Museum in Charleston to the Modjeska Monteith Simkins House in Columbia, there are numerous landmarks that highlight the struggles and achievements of African Americans in the state.

As you explore African American history in South Carolina, take the time to engage with the local communities, attend cultural events, and support African-American-owned businesses. By doing so, you are not only enriching your own travel experience but also contributing to the preservation and celebration of this important heritage.

South Carolina's African American history is a testament to resilience, determination, and the pursuit of equality. By delving into this rich tapestry, you will gain a newfound appreciation for the contributions of African Americans to the state and the nation as a whole. So, grab your guidebook, pack your bags, and embark on a journey of discovery through South Carolina's African American history.

Immersing Yourself in Southern Cuisine and Music

When it comes to experiencing the true essence of South Carolina, there are two elements that are quintessentially Southern: cuisine and music. The Palmetto State is a haven for foodies and music enthusiasts alike, offering a rich tapestry of flavors and melodies that will transport you to the heart of the South. So, if you're ready to embark on a culinary and musical adventure, prepare to immerse yourself in Southern culture like never before.

Let's start with the tantalizing world of Southern cuisine. South Carolina is renowned for its soulful dishes that reflect the region's history, traditions, and diverse influences. From Lowcountry favorites like shrimp and grits to the tangy goodness of mustard-based barbecue, there is something to satisfy every palate. Indulge in a heaping plate of fried green tomatoes, sample the flavors of Gullah cuisine, or savor the delicate flavors of she-crab soup. Don't forget to pair your meal with a glass of sweet tea, the unofficial drink of the South. And if you're feeling adventurous, why not try some fried alligator? You're in for a culinary treat!

But it's not just about the food; Southern music is the heartbeat of the region. With its roots in blues, gospel, country, and jazz, South Carolina's music scene is vibrant and diverse. From the soul-stirring melodies of the Gullah culture to the foot-stomping beats of bluegrass, you'll find yourself tapping your feet and swaying to the rhythms in no time. Be sure to catch a live performance at one of the many music venues scattered throughout the state, where you can witness the raw talent and passion of local musicians. Don't be surprised if you find yourself joining in on a line dance or two!

To fully immerse yourself in Southern cuisine and music, be sure to explore the many food and music festivals that dot the South Carolina calendar. From the Beaufort Shrimp Festival to the Charleston Food and Wine Festival, these events are a celebration of all things Southern. Savor mouth-watering dishes prepared by top chefs, listen to live performances by renowned musicians, and soak in the lively atmosphere that embodies the spirit of South Carolina.

So, whether you're a foodie, a music lover, or simply an adventurer looking to experience the rich culture of South Carolina, immersing yourself in Southern cuisine and music is an absolute must. Get ready to indulge your senses and create unforgettable memories as you journey through the flavors and melodies of the Palmetto State.

Chapter 5: Unique Experiences in South Carolina

Swamp Tours and Alligator Spotting

South Carolina is a state known for its diverse and breathtaking landscapes, and one of the most captivating natural wonders that await adventurous souls is the sprawling swamplands that dot the region. As you embark on your journey through this enchanting state, make sure to set aside time for the thrilling experience of swamp tours and alligator spotting.

Immerse yourself in the heart of nature as you glide through the mysterious and hauntingly beautiful swamps. These guided tours offer a unique opportunity to witness the intricate ecosystem that exists within these wetlands. Board a sturdy boat or hop on an airboat and let the expert guides take you on an unforgettable adventure.

As you venture deeper into the labyrinth of cypress trees and Spanish moss-draped branches, keep your eyes peeled for the ultimate thrill – spotting the fearsome alligators that call these swamps home. With their powerful presence and prehistoric charm, these ancient reptiles are sure to leave you in awe. The knowledgeable guides will share fascinating insights about these creatures, their behavior, and their vital role in maintaining the delicate balance of the ecosystem.

The swamps of South Carolina are teeming with life beyond the alligators. Keep an eye out for elegant herons, majestic bald eagles, and playful river otters as they go about their daily routines. The symphony of nature will surround you as you listen to the melodic calls of various bird species and the gentle rustling of wildlife in the undergrowth.

For those seeking a truly immersive adventure, consider exploring the swamps during the magical twilight hours. Witness the sun setting over the water, casting a golden glow that illuminates the swamps and creates an ethereal atmosphere. As darkness descends, the sounds of the nocturnal creatures fill the air, creating an otherworldly experience that will stay with you forever.

Whether you're a nature enthusiast, wildlife lover, or simply seeking an adrenaline rush, swamp tours and alligator spotting in South Carolina are an absolute must. These experiences offer a unique opportunity to connect with the untamed beauty of the region and to witness a side of nature that is both captivating and awe-inspiring.

So, grab your camera, don your adventure gear, and get ready to embark on an unforgettable journey through the captivating swamps of South Carolina. Let the magic of these wetlands enchant you as you create memories that will last a lifetime.

Ghost Tours and Haunted Places

South Carolina, a state rich in history and folklore, offers a captivating experience for tourists, adventurers, travelers, and explorers seeking an adrenaline-filled journey. Step into the realm of the supernatural as we delve into the world of ghost tours and haunted places, where history and spine-chilling tales intertwine.

Embark on a spine-tingling adventure through the dark alleyways and haunted streets of Charleston, one of the most haunted cities in America. Discover the chilling stories of Charleston's ghosts as you traverse the cobblestone streets on a guided ghost tour. Uncover the secrets of the Old Exchange Building, where restless spirits are said to roam.

Feel a shiver down your spine as you explore the eerie halls of the Old City Jail, which once housed notorious criminals and lost souls.

For those seeking a paranormal encounter, head to the legendary Magnolia Plantation and Gardens. This historic landmark is not only known for its stunning beauty but also for its ghostly inhabitants. Listen intently as the guides recount spine-chilling tales of the apparitions that are said to wander its grounds. Keep your eyes peeled for the famous ghostly figure of the "Grey Man," who appears before major hurricanes, warning residents to take shelter.

Venture further into the heart of South Carolina to explore the haunted tales of Columbia. Join a haunted walking tour through the historic district, where you'll hear the chilling accounts of spirits that still linger in the city's oldest buildings. Visit the South Carolina State Hospital, better known as the "Bull Street Asylum," where ghostly whispers and unexplained phenomena have been reported by many.

Suppose you're up for an eerie escapade, a journey to the coastal city of Beaufort, where the spirits of the past beckon you. Explore the haunted Beaufort Arsenal, where apparitions and strange occurrences have puzzled visitors for years. Stroll through the historic district, where stories of vengeful spirits and haunted homes will send shivers down your spine.

Whether you're a history enthusiast or a thrill-seeker, South Carolina's ghost tours and haunted places offer an unforgettable and spine-chilling experience. Prepare to be captivated by the tales of restless spirits and the mysteries that lie within the historic walls of this enchanting state.

So, gather your courage, step into the unknown, and let the ghosts of South Carolina guide you through an adventure unlike any other. Experience the eerie side of this beautiful state and uncover the secrets that await in the shadows. Explore South Carolina's haunted past and create memories that will haunt your dreams for years to come.

*Please note that the information provided in this guide is accurate as of 2024-2025. However, we recommend checking the availability and schedules of ghost tours and haunted places before planning your visit.

Discovering the World of Barbecue in South Carolina

South Carolina, known for its rich history and stunning natural beauty, has another aspect that will tantalize your senses - its unique and mouthwatering barbecue traditions. For tourists, adventurers, travelers, and explorers seeking an unforgettable culinary experience, a journey into the world of barbecue in South Carolina is an absolute must.

South Carolina boasts a diverse barbecue scene, with each region offering its own distinct flavors and techniques. From the savory mustard-based sauces of the Midlands to the tangy vinegar and pepper concoctions of the Lowcountry, there's something to satisfy every palate. Embark on a gastronomic adventure as you explore the state's barbecue hotspots.

Start your journey in the Midlands, where you'll find a blend of classic and innovative barbecue. Sink your teeth into slow-cooked pulled pork smothered in tangy mustard-based sauce, a unique tradition that sets South Carolina apart from other barbecue hubs. Visit local barbecue joints and traditional smokehouses, where pitmasters proudly showcase their craft passed down through generations.

Next, venture to the Lowcountry, home to a distinctly different barbecue style. Here, you'll discover the mouthwatering flavors of vinegar and pepper-based sauces that perfectly complement slow-cooked pork. Indulge in whole hog barbecue, a tradition that involves pit-roasting the entire pig until it reaches unparalleled tenderness. Be sure to pair your meal with classic Southern sides like collard greens, cornbread, and hush puppies.

For those seeking a taste of the coast, head to the Pee Dee region. Here, you'll find a fusion of barbecue styles influenced by both the Midlands and Lowcountry. Savor the smoky flavors of slow-cooked meats and explore the unique variations of sauces that combine the best of both worlds.

To truly immerse yourself in the world of South Carolina barbecue, don't miss the annual barbecue festivals held throughout the state. These lively events celebrate the art of barbecue, featuring mouthwatering dishes, live music, and friendly competitions among pitmasters. Get a taste of the local culture and witness the passion that goes into creating these delectable dishes.

Whether you're a seasoned barbecue connoisseur or a curious traveler looking to expand your culinary horizons, South Carolina's barbecue scene promises an unforgettable adventure. Indulge in the flavors, embrace the traditions, and uncover the stories behind this beloved Southern cuisine. Your taste buds will thank you as you discover the world of barbecue in South Carolina, a journey that will leave you craving for more.

Exploring the Unique Beaches of South Carolina

Welcome to the picturesque coastline of South Carolina, where sun-kissed shores meet the vast Atlantic Ocean. As you embark on your adventure through the Palmetto State, prepare to be captivated by the unique and diverse beaches that await you. Whether you are a tourist, adventurer, traveler, or explorer, this subchapter will be your ultimate guide to discovering the hidden gems along South Carolina's coastline.

1. Hilton Head Island: Nestled on the southernmost tip of the state, Hilton Head Island offers a pristine beach experience like no other. With its white sandy shores, crystal-clear waters, and lush greenery, this island paradise is a haven for water sports enthusiasts, nature lovers, and relaxation seekers alike.

2. Myrtle Beach: Known as the "Grand Strand," Myrtle Beach is a bustling hub of entertainment and natural beauty. Stretching over 60 miles, this beach destination offers endless opportunities for family fun, from amusement parks and water sports to shopping and dining. Don't miss the iconic Myrtle Beach Boardwalk, where you can soak up the vibrant atmosphere and stunning ocean views.

3. Kiawah Island: For a serene and secluded beach getaway, Kiawah Island is the perfect choice. This barrier island boasts untouched landscapes, pristine sandy beaches, and abundant wildlife. Take a leisurely stroll along the shore, go bird-watching, or tee off at one of the island's world-class golf courses.

4. Folly Beach: If you're seeking a laid-back and bohemian vibe, Folly Beach is where you'll find it. Known as the "Edge of America," this charming beach town offers a vibrant mix of surf culture, eclectic shops, and delicious seafood. Catch a wave, explore the iconic Folly Beach Pier, or simply unwind with a breathtaking sunset.

5. Hunting Island State Park: Nature enthusiasts will be enthralled by the natural wonders of Hunting Island State Park. Located near Beaufort, this untouched paradise boasts pristine beaches, maritime forests, and the iconic Hunting Island Lighthouse. Hike along the trails, go fishing, or camp under the starry skies for an unforgettable experience.

As you explore the unique beaches of South Carolina, be sure to immerse yourself in the rich history, vibrant culture, and warm hospitality that this coastal state has to offer. From charming beach towns to untouched natural wonders, South Carolina's coastline is a treasure trove waiting to be discovered.

Festival and Event Highlights in South Carolina

South Carolina is a vibrant state filled with rich history, stunning landscapes, and a lively culture. One of the best ways to immerse yourself in the local scene and experience the true essence of the Palmetto State is by attending its numerous festivals and events. From music and arts to food and history, South Carolina offers something for every traveler, adventurer, and explorer. In this subchapter, we will explore the must-visit festivals and events that will make your trip to South Carolina an unforgettable adventure.

1. Spoleto Festival USA: Held annually in Charleston, the Spoleto Festival USA is a world-renowned event celebrating the performing arts. For 17 days, the city comes alive with opera, theater, dance, and music performances, attracting artists and spectators from around the globe.

2. South Carolina State Fair: Get ready for fun, excitement, and mouthwatering treats at the South Carolina State Fair. Held in Columbia, this event showcases thrilling rides, live entertainment, competitive exhibits, and delicious fair food that will satisfy any foodie's cravings.

3. Charleston Food and Wine Festival: Calling all food lovers! Indulge in the culinary delights of the Lowcountry at the Charleston Food and Wine Festival. Explore the diverse flavors of South Carolina through tastings, cooking demonstrations, wine seminars, and exclusive dining experiences.

4. Gullah Festival: Immerse yourself in the unique Gullah culture, a vibrant African-American community with deep roots in South Carolina, at the annual Gullah Festival in Beaufort. Enjoy traditional music, dance, crafts, and authentic Gullah cuisine while learning about the rich heritage of this fascinating community.

5. Myrtle Beach Bike Week: Rev up your engines and join the excitement of Myrtle Beach Bike Week, one of the largest motorcycle rallies on the East Coast. Feel the thrill as thousands of bikers gather to showcase their rides, enjoy live music, and explore the beautiful coastal roads of South Carolina.

6. South Carolina Peach Festival: Celebrate the sweetest fruit of the South at the South Carolina Peach Festival in Gaffney. This family-friendly event features peach-themed activities, live music, arts and crafts, and, of course, plenty of juicy peaches to indulge in.

7. Beaufort Water Festival: Dive into the coastal culture of South Carolina at the Beaufort Water Festival. This week-long event offers a variety of water sports, live entertainment, boat parades, and fireworks, all set against the stunning backdrop of Beaufort's waterfront.

These are just a few of the many festivals and events that showcase the diverse and vibrant culture of South Carolina. Whether you're a history buff, a music enthusiast, a foodie, or simply seeking a unique adventure, South Carolina will captivate your senses and leave you with memories to treasure. Plan your visit to coincide with these incredible festivals and events, and get ready to experience the best that South Carolina has to offer.

Chapter 6: Practical Travel Information

Transportation Options in South Carolina

South Carolina, with its stunning landscapes and vibrant cities, offers a plethora of transportation options for tourists, adventurers, travelers, and explorers alike. Whether you're planning a scenic road trip or seeking convenient ways to navigate the state's attractions, South Carolina has you covered with its diverse transportation network.

1. Renting a Car: For those who crave the freedom to explore at their own pace, renting a car is an excellent choice. With numerous rental agencies available at major airports and cities like Charleston and Columbia, you can easily find a vehicle that suits your needs. From the majestic Blue Ridge Mountains to the picturesque coastline, having a car allows you to discover South Carolina's hidden gems.

2. Public Transportation: South Carolina boasts an efficient public transportation system, making it easy to travel between cities and towns. The Palmetto Breeze buses connect various destinations, including Charleston, Myrtle Beach, and Hilton Head Island. Additionally, the CARTA bus system operates in Charleston, providing convenient access to the city's attractions.

3. Amtrak: If you prefer train travel, Amtrak offers several routes that pass through South Carolina. The Silver Meteor and Palmetto lines stop at cities like Charleston, Columbia, and Florence, allowing you to enjoy the scenic beauty of the state from the comfort of a train.

4. Air Travel: South Carolina is well-served by several major airports, making it a convenient destination for air travelers. The Charleston International Airport, Columbia Metropolitan Airport, and Greenville-Spartanburg International Airport offer frequent flights to various domestic and international destinations. Once you arrive, renting a car or utilizing public transportation will help you reach your desired location.

5. Cycling: For adventurous souls who prefer eco-friendly and active modes of transportation, cycling is a popular choice in South Carolina. With its picturesque landscapes and numerous bike-friendly routes, the state offers an excellent opportunity to explore its natural beauty while getting some exercise.

6. Ferries and Boats: South Carolina's stunning coastline and vast waterways make ferries and boats a unique transportation option. From Charleston, you can take a ferry to explore the beautiful beaches of Sullivan's Island or take a boat tour to witness the incredible wildlife in the coastal areas.

Whether you prefer the freedom of a car, the convenience of public transportation, or the adventure of cycling, South Carolina offers transportation options to suit every traveler's needs. So, embark on your ultimate adventure in South Carolina and experience the charm of this extraordinary state in the most convenient and exciting way possible.

Accommodation Choices for Every Budget

When planning a trip to South Carolina, one of the most important aspects to consider is where to stay. Luckily, the Palmetto State offers a wide range of accommodation choices to suit every budget. Whether you're a luxury traveler or a budget-conscious backpacker, there's something for everyone in this charming southern destination.

For those seeking the ultimate indulgence, South Carolina boasts a plethora of high-end resorts and luxury hotels. From beachfront properties in Hilton Head Island to historical mansions in Charleston, these accommodations offer lavish amenities, impeccable service, and stunning views. Pamper yourself with spa treatments, enjoy fine dining experiences, and relax in opulent surroundings. Your stay in South Carolina will be nothing short of extraordinary.

If you're looking for a mid-range option, consider the numerous boutique hotels and bed and breakfasts scattered throughout the state. These charming and often historic establishments provide a unique and personalized experience. Stay in beautifully restored Victorian houses, quaint cottages, or cozy inns, and immerse yourself in the local culture. Many of these establishments offer complimentary breakfasts and amenities that guarantee a comfortable stay without breaking the bank.

For the budget-conscious traveler, South Carolina offers a variety of affordable accommodation options. Motels, budget hotels, and hostels can be found in popular tourist destinations such as Myrtle Beach and Columbia. These accommodations provide clean and comfortable rooms at a fraction of the cost, allowing you to stretch your travel budget further. While they may not have all the luxuries of higher-end options, they are perfect for those who prioritize exploring the destination rather than spending time in their room.

For the adventurous souls, South Carolina also offers unique options such as camping and RV parks. Explore the stunning state parks, pitch your tent under the stars, or park your RV amidst beautiful natural surroundings. Wake up to the sound of birds chirping and enjoy breathtaking views while being immersed in nature. Camping is not only a budget-friendly option, but it also allows you to experience South Carolina's incredible outdoor offerings up close and personal.

No matter your budget or travel style, South Carolina has accommodation choices that will suit your needs. From luxurious resorts to cozy bed and breakfasts, there's something for everyone. So, start planning your adventure and make the most out of your visit to this captivating southern state.

Budget Hotels in South Carolina

Economic and Accessible Places to Lodge in South Carolina

Planning a trip to South Carolina? The state offers something for everyone. Wondering if there are budget-friendly hotels in South Carolina? Absolutely! We've evaluated the most affordable accommodations in the state, considering factors like price, amenities, location, activities, and guest reviews.

Our aim? To unearth the best deals and low-cost hotels in South Carolina that offer more than just a place to sleep. Whether you're a seasoned traveler or new to the area, here's how to find economical lodging in South Carolina.

You don't have to sacrifice comfort or amenities to save money on accommodation, as many of these hotels offer excellent features and amenities without breaking the bank. Even modest motels can offer pleasant surprises if you know where to look.

Saving on lodging means more funds for activities, sightseeing, shopping, and dining out. When seeking a bargain hotel, you'll likely be interested in amenities like a pool, parking, extra space, complimentary breakfast, and more.

Many of these budget-friendly hotels provide such amenities and much more. Keep reading to discover where to stay affordably in South Carolina and the actual costs of these great deals.

(Prices are shown in U.S. Dollars. Book hotels on Kayak or Booking.com)

1. Hilton Garden Inn Myrtle Beach/Coastal Grand Mall

- Myrtle Beach, South Carolina
- 3-star Hotel with rates starting at $119 (excluding taxes)

- An Exceptional Budget-Friendly Hotel
  - Excellent Value: Rates are below average for 3-star hotels.
  - Ideal for Families
  - Features an Outdoor Pool
  - Pool is Heated

Situated at 2383 Coastal Grand Circle, Hilton Garden Inn Myrtle Beach/Coastal Grand Mall offers fantastic rooms from $119 (before taxes). The Hotel boasts an outdoor pool, room service, an on-site restaurant, a fitness center, and a bar.

With an impressive rating of 8.60 out of 10 from previous guests, this Hotel is a hit. Located only 120.9 miles from the city center, budget-conscious travelers will appreciate amenities such as a kid-friendly buffet, laundry services, pet-friendly rooms, a hot tub, and an indoor pool.

You can enjoy the convenience of room service while staying here. With rates lower than the average for budget hotels, this Hotel provides excellent value.

Budget Hotel Features

- Outdoor Pool
- Indoor Pool
- Free Parking
- Laundry Facilities
- Budget-Friendly

- **Additional Amenities**
  - Restaurant

- Fitness Center
- Bar/Lounge
- Kid-Friendly Buffet
- Laundry Service
- Pet-Friendly
- Hot Tub
- Family Rooms
- Heated Pool
- Air Conditioning
- Microwave
- Refrigerator
- Family-Friendly

2. SpringHill Suites Charleston North/Ashley Phosphate

- Charleston, South Carolina
- 3-star Hotel with rates starting at $101 (excluding taxes)

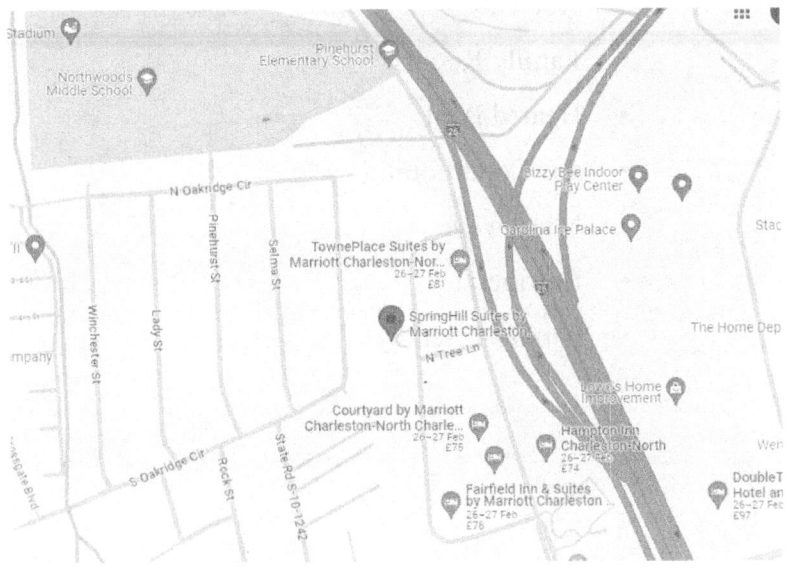

- A Highly Affordable Accommodation
    - Excellent Value: Rates are below average for 3-star hotels.

Consider staying at SpringHill Suites Charleston North/Ashley Phosphate, offering pleasant rooms starting at $101. This Hotel provides room service, a fitness center, a kid-friendly buffet, breakfast, and child care. With a commendable guest rating of 8.30 out of 10, it's located at 7535 North Forest Drive. This peaceful Hotel offers laundry services, complimentary breakfast, an indoor pool, free parking, and laundry facilities. Moreover, it's just 91.4 miles from the city center. The indoor pool is a delightful feature, providing a great spot for relaxation and fun, regardless of the weather. With rates below the average for budget hotels, this establishment offers exceptional value.

Budget Hotel Features

- Complimentary Breakfast
- Indoor Pool
- Free Parking
- Laundry Facilities
- Budget-Friendly

- **Additional Amenities**
  - Fitness Center
  - Kid-Friendly Buffet
  - Breakfast Included
  - Laundry Service
  - Family Rooms
  - Air Conditioning

- Microwave
- Refrigerator

3. **Courtyard by Marriott Myrtle Beach Barefoot Landing Myrtle Beach**

- Myrtle Beach, South Carolina
- 3-star Hotel with rates starting at $100 (before taxes)

- An Excellent Budget-Friendly Hotel
    - Excellent Value: Rates are below average for 3-star hotels.

- Perfect for Families
- Features an Indoor Pool

We've found Courtyard by Marriott Myrtle Beach Barefoot Landing Myrtle Beach to be an excellent choice, with rates starting at $100. This Hotel offers room service, a restaurant, a fitness center, a bar, and childcare services, garnering a remarkable guest rating of 8.10 out of 10.

Situated at 1000 Commons Boulevard, the Hotel also provides laundry services, golfing opportunities, pet-friendly rooms, a hot tub, and an indoor pool, making it a favorite among travelers. At just 129.7 miles from the city center, it's a convenient spot to unwind after a day of exploration.

Dining at the hotel restaurant post-sightseeing adds a delightful touch to your stay. Additionally, with rates lower than the average for budget hotels, this establishment offers exceptional value.

Budget Hotel Amenities

- Indoor Pool

- Free Parking
- Laundry Facilities
- Budget-Friendly
- **Additional Amenities**
  - Restaurant
  - Fitness Center
  - Bar/Lounge
  - Laundry Service
  - Pets Allowed
  - Hot Tub
  - Air Conditioning
  - Microwave

- **Hyatt Place Charleston Airport / Convention Center**
- Charleston, South Carolina
- 3-star Hotel with rates starting at $132 (before taxes)

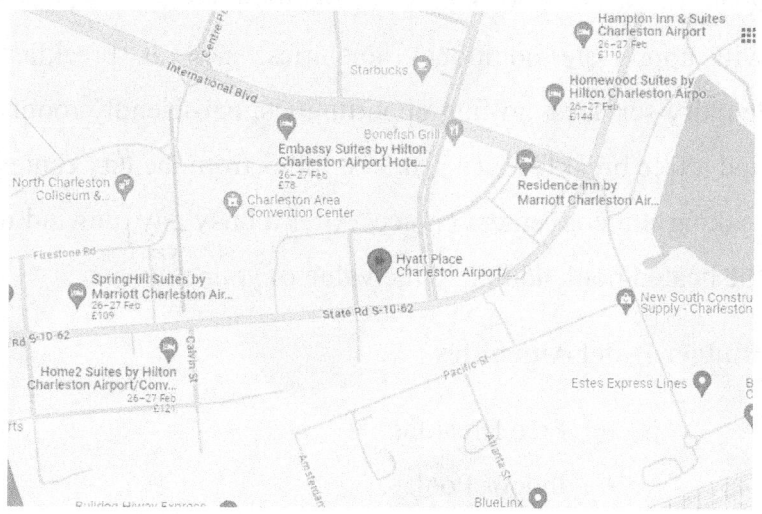

- A Pleasant Budget Retreat
    - Excellent Value: Rates are below average for 3-star hotels.
    - Family-Friendly
    - Features a Heated Pool

With fantastic rooms starting at $132, Hyatt Place Charleston Airport / Convention Center, located at 3234 W Montague Ave, offers room service, a restaurant, a fitness center, a bar, and a kid-friendly buffet. With an impressive guest rating of 8.60 out of 10, budget-conscious travelers will appreciate additional amenities such as breakfast, laundry services, golfing opportunities, pet-friendly rooms, and a free breakfast. It's just 96.8 miles from the city center, making it a convenient choice. After a busy day, unwind in the heated pool, adding to the value of your stay.

Budget Hotel Amenities

- Free Breakfast
- Indoor Pool
- Free Parking
- Laundry Facilities
- Budget-Friendly

- **Additional Amenities**
  - Restaurant
  - Fitness Center
  - Bar/Lounge
  - Kid-Friendly Buffet
  - Breakfast Included

- Laundry Service
- Pets Allowed
- Family Rooms
- Heated Pool
- Air Conditioning
- Refrigerator

4. **Towers At North Myrtle Beach**

- Myrtle Beach, South Carolina
- 2-star Hotel with rates starting at $85 (before taxes)

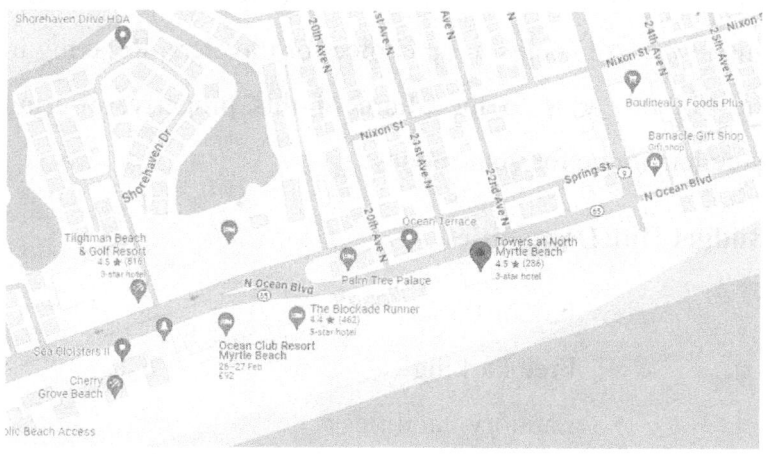

- One of the Best Bargains in South Carolina
    - Excellent Value: Rates are below average for 2-star hotels.
    - Beachfront Property

- Features a Heated Pool

With a superb guest rating of 8.00 out of 10, Towers At North Myrtle Beach offers a fitness center, rooms with kitchens or kitchenettes, golfing opportunities, and city views. Rooms start at $85 before taxes and vary depending on the season.

Located at 2100 North Ocean Blvd, the Hotel also boasts a hot tub, an indoor pool, free parking, laundry facilities, and family-friendly rooms. Just 135.5 miles from the city center, this low-cost Hotel is a top choice for travelers. Relaxing in the hot tub adds to the allure of this property, offering excellent value for your money.

Budget Hotel Amenities

- Indoor Pool
- Free Parking
- Laundry Facilities
- Beachfront Property
- Budget-Friendly

- **Additional Amenities**
    - Fitness Center
    - Kitchen

- Kitchenette
- Hot Tub
- Family Rooms
- Heated Pool
- Air Conditioning
- Microwave
- Refrigerator

5. Holiday Inn Express and Suites North Charleston

- Charleston, South Carolina
- 2-star Hotel with rates starting at $148 (before taxes)

- An Exceptional Deal in South Carolina
  - Excellent Value: Rates are below average for budget hotels.
  - Family-Friendly

With a remarkable guest rating of 8.70 out of 10, Holiday Inn Express and Suites North Charleston offers a fitness center, a kid-friendly buffet, breakfast, rooms with kitchenettes, and laundry services. Rates for the fantastic rooms start at $148, and it's located at 3025 West Montague Avenue. Additional amenities include free breakfast, a hot tub, a spa, an indoor pool, and free parking, making it an excellent choice for travelers. At just 96.8 miles from the city center, it boasts a convenient location.

Being able to prepare food in your room adds to the convenience of your stay. With rates lower than the average for budget hotels, this property provides exceptional value.

Budget Hotel Amenities

- Free Breakfast
- Indoor Pool
- Free Parking
- Laundry Facilities
- Budget-Friendly
- **Additional Amenities**
  - Fitness Center
  - Kid-Friendly Buffet
  - Breakfast Included
  - Kitchenette

- Laundry Service
- Hot Tub
- Air Conditioning
- Microwave
- Refrigerator
- Family-Friendly

6. Wingate by Wyndham Charleston Southern University

Charleston, South Carolina

3-star Hotel with rates starting at $138 (excluding taxes) –

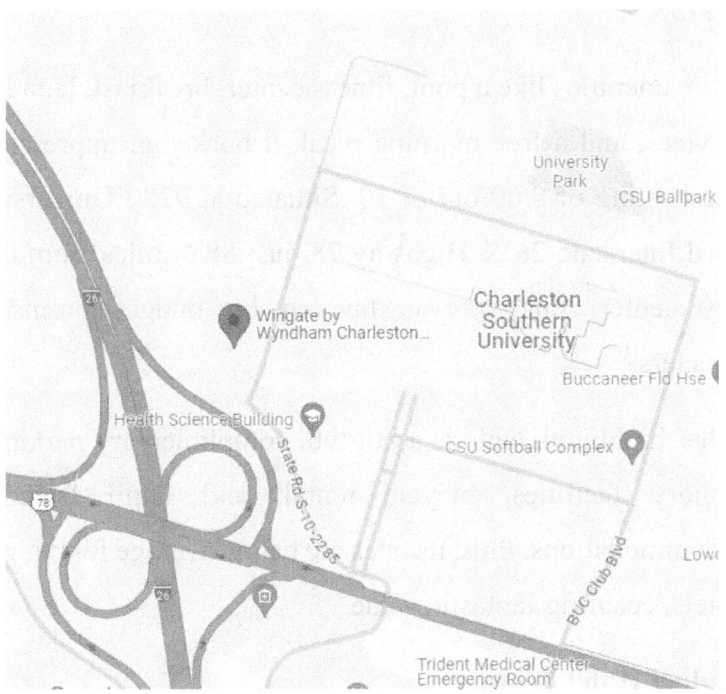

- Exceptional Value in South Carolina
    - Tremendous Value: Rates below the norm for 3-star hotels.
    - Ideal for Families

- Pool

Discover the inviting Wingate by Wyndham Charleston Southern University, which offers excellent rooms starting at $138.

With amenities like a pool, fitness center, breakfast, laundry services, and a free morning meal, it boasts an impressive guest rating of 8.60 out of 10. Situated at 9280 University Blvd Interstate 26 & Highway 78, just 88.6 miles from the city center, this spot is favored by budget-conscious travelers.

Other highlights include a hot tub, complimentary parking, laundry facilities, bicycle rental, and family-friendly accommodations. Plus, its rates are below average for budget hotels, ensuring fantastic value.

Budget Hotel Features

- Free breakfast
- Free parking
- Laundry facilities
- Budget-Friendly

- **Additional Amenities**
  - Pool
  - Fitness center
  - Complimentary breakfast
  - Laundry service
  - Hot tub
  - Bicycle rental
  - Family rooms
  - Air-conditioned
  - Microwave
  - Refrigerator
  - Family-Friendly

7. **Fairfield Inn & Suites by Marriott Charleston North/Ashley Phosphate**
- Charleston, South Carolina
- 2-star Hotel with rates starting at $106 (excluding taxes)

- Top-notch Affordable Accommodations in South Carolina
    - Excellent Value: Rates below the norm for 2-star hotels.
    - Outdoor Pool

Fairfield Inn & Suites by Marriott Charleston North/Ashley Phosphate offers an outdoor pool, fitness center, kid-friendly buffet, breakfast, and childcare services.

Rooms start at a remarkable $106 (before taxes) and boast an 8.10/10 guest rating. Found at 2540 North Forest Drive, this serene Hotel also provides laundry services, complimentary breakfast, pet-friendly rooms, free parking, and laundry facilities. Situated just 91.7 miles from the city center, it's a perfect spot for a refreshing swim and relaxation. And with rates lower than the average for budget hotels, it's a steal.

Budget Hotel Features

- Outdoor pool
- Free breakfast
- Free parking
- Laundry facilities
- Budget-Friendly

- **Additional Amenities**
  - Fitness center
  - Kid-friendly buffet
  - Complimentary breakfast
  - Laundry service
  - Pets allowed
  - Air-conditioned
  - Microwave

- Refrigerator
- Airport shuttle

8. The Horizon at 77th

Myrtle Beach, South Carolina

3-star Hotel with rates starting at $125 (excluding taxes)

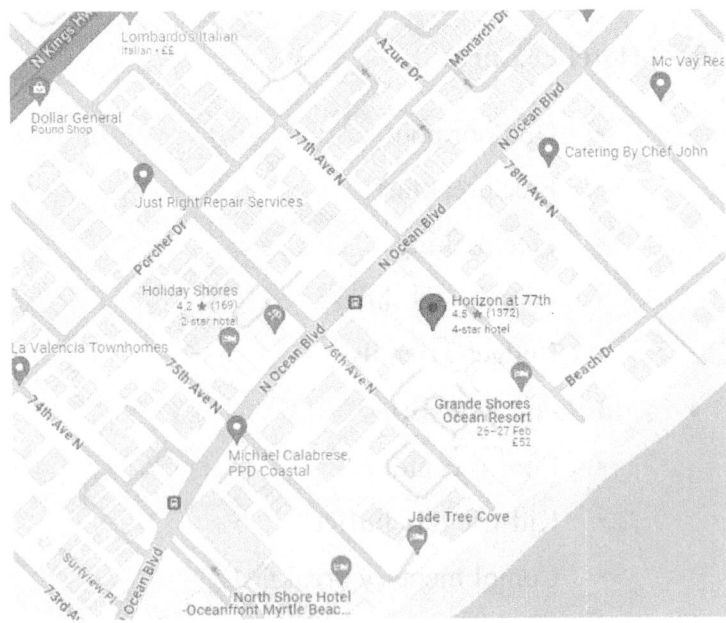

- Terrific Value Hotel
    - Great Value: Rates below the norm for 3-star hotels.

- Beachfront
- Family-Oriented
- Outdoor Pool
- Heated Pool

Nestled at 215 77th Avenue North, The Horizon at 77th offers fantastic rooms from $125 (before taxes). With an outdoor pool, fitness center, kitchen-equipped rooms, city views, and golfing options, it's earned a commendable 8.40 guest rating. Guests will also appreciate the hot tub, spa, child pool, and indoor pool.

Only 126.6 miles from the city center, it's an ideal choice for a relaxing beach vacation. And with a kitchenette in the room, guests can prepare meals conveniently. Plus, its rates are lower than average for budget hotels, ensuring exceptional value.

Budget Hotel Features

- Outdoor pool
- Child pool
- Indoor pool
- Free parking

- Laundry facilities
- Beach Access
- Budget-Friendly
- **Additional Amenities**
  - Fitness center
  - Kitchenette
  - Hot tub
  - Family rooms
  - Heated pool
  - Air-conditioned
  - Microwave
  - Refrigerator
  - Family-Friendly

9. Comfort Suites West of the Ashley

- Charleston, South Carolina
- 3-star Hotel with rates starting at $114 (excluding taxes)

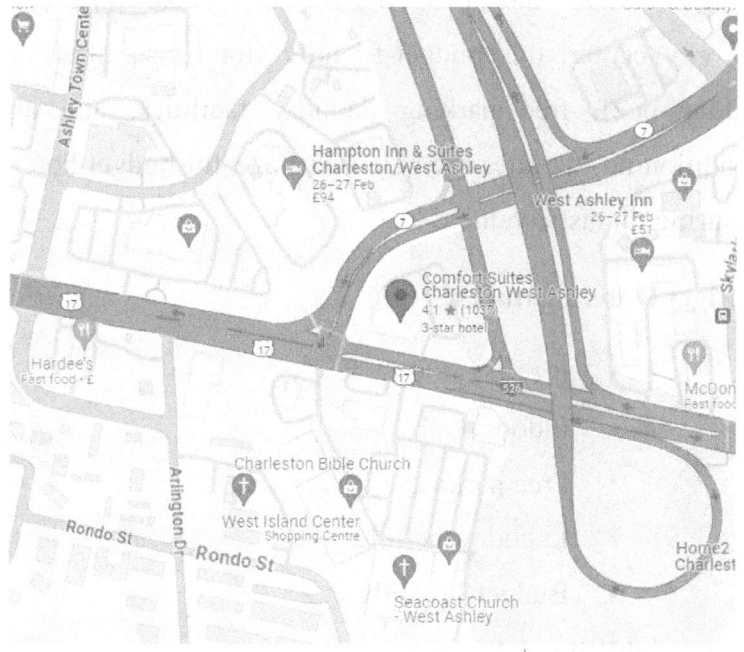

- Affordable and Family-Friendly
    - Excellent Value: Rates below the norm for 3-star hotels.
    - Heated Pool

Comfort Suites West of the Ashley offers cozy rooms starting at $114. Featuring a fitness center, breakfast, kitchenette-equipped rooms, laundry services, and complimentary breakfast, it boasts an 8.30 guest rating. Situated at 2080 Savannah Highway, just 100.6 miles from the city center, this budget-friendly Hotel also offers an indoor pool, free parking, laundry facilities, and air-conditioning. Its rates are below average for budget hotels, ensuring fantastic value.

Budget Hotel Features

- Free breakfast
- Indoor pool
- Free parking
- Laundry facilities
- Budget-Friendly

- **Additional Amenities**
  - Fitness center
  - Complimentary breakfast
  - Kitchenette
  - Laundry service
  - Heated pool
  - Air-conditioned

- Microwave
- Refrigerator
- Family-Friendly

Dining and Local Cuisine Recommendations

South Carolina, a state known for its rich history and diverse culture, provides an array of dining options that will tantalize your taste buds and leave you craving for more. From traditional Southern comfort food to innovative culinary creations, the local cuisine in South Carolina offers a delightful gastronomic adventure for all tourists, adventurers, travelers, and explorers.

When it comes to Southern cuisine, South Carolina proudly boasts its famous Lowcountry dishes. One must not miss the opportunity to savor the delectable shrimp and grits, a classic combination of fresh local shrimp and creamy stone-ground grits. For those seeking a taste of true Southern charm, indulge in a plate of succulent fried chicken paired with collard greens and cornbread, a true staple of the region.

For seafood lovers, South Carolina's coastal areas offer an abundance of fresh catch. The renowned Charleston crab cakes, made with lump crab meat and seasoned to perfection, are a must-try delicacy. Another coastal favorite is she-crab soup, a creamy bisque made with crab roe and delicate spices, providing a luxurious and indulgent experience.

In addition to its traditional Southern fare, South Carolina also embraces a diverse culinary scene. The city of Charleston, often regarded as a food lover's paradise, offers a vibrant array of restaurants and cafes. From farm-to-table establishments to fusion cuisine, Charleston's culinary landscape is a haven for food enthusiasts. Be sure to try the mouthwatering dishes at Husk, where the menu highlights Southern ingredients in innovative and creative ways.

For those seeking a taste of South Carolina's barbecue culture, head to the upstate region. Here, you'll find a variety of barbecue joints offering smoky and flavorful meats cooked low and slow. From pulled pork sandwiches to tender ribs, these establishments are sure to satisfy your carnivorous cravings.

To truly immerse yourself in the local cuisine, consider visiting one of South Carolina's many farmers' markets. These markets showcase the state's agricultural bounty, offering fresh produce, artisanal cheeses, and homemade preserves. Engaging with local vendors and tasting their offerings will provide an authentic and unique experience.

Whether you're a foodie or simply looking to explore the culinary wonders of South Carolina, the state's dining scene will undoubtedly leave you with unforgettable memories. From traditional Southern favorites to cutting-edge gastronomy, the local cuisine in South Carolina is a true reflection of its rich history and cultural diversity.

So, embark on a culinary journey and discover the flavors that make South Carolina a destination for food lovers from around the world.

Safety Tips for Traveling in South Carolina

When embarking on an adventure in the beautiful state of South Carolina, it is important to prioritize your safety and well-being. With its diverse landscapes, historic sites, and vibrant culture, South Carolina offers an array of exciting experiences for tourists, adventurers, travelers, and explorers alike. To ensure a smooth and worry-free journey, here are some essential safety tips to keep in mind:

1. Stay Informed: Before you embark on your South Carolina adventure, research the destination thoroughly.

Stay updated on local news, weather conditions, and any potential safety concerns. The South Carolina Department of Natural Resources and the National Park Service are excellent sources of information regarding outdoor activities and wildlife encounters.

2. Carry Essentials: Always carry a map, a fully charged mobile phone, and a first aid kit. These essentials can prove invaluable during emergencies or unexpected situations. It is also advisable to keep a list of emergency contacts, including the local authorities and your embassy or consulate.

3. Be Weather-ready: South Carolina experiences a range of weather conditions throughout the year. Whether you're exploring the coastal regions, hiking through the mountains, or venturing into the swamps, be prepared for sudden changes in weather. Pack appropriate clothing layers, sunscreen, insect repellent, and plenty of water to stay hydrated.

4. Practice Water Safety: South Carolina's extensive coastline and numerous lakes offer ample opportunities for water-based activities. However, it's essential to prioritize water safety. Whether you're swimming, boating, or participating in water sports, always wear a life jacket, swim in designated areas, and be cautious of strong currents or undertows.

5. Wildlife Awareness: South Carolina is home to diverse wildlife, including alligators, snakes, and other potentially dangerous animals. While encountering wildlife can be exciting, maintain a safe distance and never attempt to feed or approach them. Familiarize yourself with local wildlife and follow any guidelines provided by authorities.

6. Stay Alert in Urban Areas: While South Carolina is generally a safe destination, it is always wise to exercise caution in urban areas. Keep an eye on your belongings, avoid walking alone at night in unfamiliar places, and be aware of your surroundings. It is advisable to use reputable transportation services and stay in well-lit areas.

By adhering to these safety tips, you can fully enjoy your South Carolina adventure while minimizing risks and ensuring a memorable experience. Remember, exploring South Carolina is a journey filled with beauty, history, and thrilling experiences, and by prioritizing your safety, you can make the most of your travels in this captivating state.

Essential Packing List for Adventurers

When embarking on an adventurous journey to South Carolina, it is crucial to pack the right gear and essentials to ensure an unforgettable and hassle-free experience. Whether you are a seasoned adventurer or a first-time explorer, this essential packing list will equip you with everything you need to make the most of your trip to the beautiful state of South Carolina.

1. Comfortable Clothing: Pack lightweight and breathable clothing suitable for the region's warm and humid climate. Include a mix of shorts, t-shirts, long-sleeved shirts, and pants for versatility. Don't forget a waterproof jacket and a hat for protection against sudden weather changes.

2. Footwear: South Carolina offers a diverse range of terrains, so pack sturdy and comfortable footwear. Bring hiking boots for trails, water shoes for aquatic adventures, and sandals for casual strolls along the coast.

3. Outdoor Gear: If you're an outdoor enthusiast, ensure you have the necessary equipment. This includes a backpack, hiking poles, a compass, binoculars, a multi-tool, and a headlamp. These items will come in handy during hikes, wildlife spotting, and exploring South Carolina's breathtaking landscapes.

4. Protection against the Elements: South Carolina's sunny weather calls for sun protection essentials. Pack sunscreen with a high SPF, sunglasses, and a wide-brimmed hat. Additionally, insect repellent is essential to ward off pesky bugs during outdoor activities.

5. Water Bottles and Snacks: Stay hydrated during your adventures by bringing refillable water bottles. South Carolina offers numerous natural springs and water sources, and having a water filtration system or purification tablets is highly recommended. Additionally, pack energy bars and snacks to keep your energy levels up during long hikes or excursions.

6. Maps and Guidebooks: Familiarize yourself with South Carolina's rich history and diverse landscapes by carrying guidebooks and maps. These resources will help you navigate the region, discover hidden gems, and make the most of your time in the state.

7. Camera and Binoculars: Capture the magnificent beauty of South Carolina's wildlife and landscapes with a quality camera. Additionally, binoculars will enhance your wildlife spotting experience, allowing you to observe rare bird species and other wildlife from a distance.

Remember, this essential packing list is tailored for adventurers visiting South Carolina. Adjust it according to your personal preferences and the activities you plan to engage in. Whether you're exploring the stunning coastal regions, hiking through the picturesque mountains, or immersing yourself in the rich culture and history of the state, having the right gear and essentials will enhance your experience and ensure a memorable adventure in South Carolina.

Chapter 7: 6 Day trip from Charleston

Five-day trips from Charleston to capture the best of South Carolina

Nestled amidst coastal islands, centuries-old historic sites, and wildlife-rich parks, Charleston serves as an ideal launching point for captivating day excursions—provided you've indulged in the delights of chef-driven eateries and rooftop cocktails, naturally.

From leisurely strolls through swampy forests to paddling across salt marshes or immersing oneself in Gullah culture, this curated selection of top-day trips caters to a diverse range of travelers. Given the impracticality of public transportation, reaching these destinations typically requires a car journey or, in certain instances, participation in an organized tour.

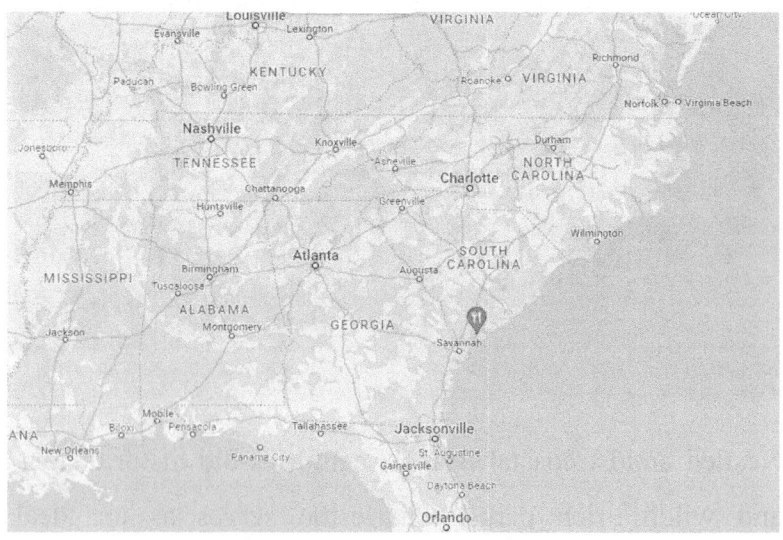

Visit to Beaufort & the Lowcountry

Indulge in a captivating blend of history and nature with a visit to Beaufort & the Lowcountry.

For a setting reminiscent of a movie backdrop and a vibrant celebration of Gullah culture, venture southward to Beaufort (pronounced Byoo-furt) and its neighboring islands.

Perched on Port Royal Island, Beaufort enchants visitors with its picturesque riverside setting, where avenues are flanked by antebellum homes and majestic magnolia trees. The quaint downtown area buzzes with charming cafes and art galleries.

Notable films such as The Big Chill, The Great Santini, and Forrest Gump have graced this historic locale with their presence.

Just east lies a cluster of marshy, rural islands, among which St. Helena Island shines as the heart of Gullah country. Here, descendants of enslaved West Africans diligently preserve their rich cultural heritage.

The historic Penn Center, one of the earliest schools for emancipated slaves, now houses a museum chronicling its significant history.

Adjacent to the Penn Center lies Hunting Island State Park, boasting a mesmerizing maritime forest crisscrossed by scenic trails. Its marshlands and saltwater lagoon serve as prime locations for observing wildlife, while the pristine white sand beach beckons beachcombers to scan for seashells.

To embark on this enriching journey, travel 70 miles south of Charleston via U.S. 17 S and U.S. 21 S to reach Beaufort. Continue your southward journey on U.S. 21, also known as the Sea Island Parkway, to access St. Helena Island and Hunting Island State Park, where nature and history converge in a breathtaking tapestry of experiences.

Tour the Ashley River Plantations

Three significant sites north of Charleston provide a profound opportunity to confront and understand the troubling legacy of slavery in the United States.

While we highly recommend these locations for their insightful discussions on the institution of slavery, their present-day grounds are meticulously maintained, with the iconic live oaks adorned in Spanish moss evoking a sense of Southern Gothic ambiance.

Leading the lineup is Drayton Hall, a Palladian brick house completed in 1738, marking it as the oldest unrestored plantation house in the nation accessible to the public. The sprawling Magnolia Plantation offers a more commercial experience, featuring a tram, zoo, and guided house tour. However, its swamp garden trail offers a serene escape, with alligators occasionally sighted in the surrounding wilderness.

Designed in 1741, the elegant and expansive gardens at Middleton Place stand as the oldest landscaped gardens in the United States. Visitors can savor delectable Lowcountry cuisine at Middleton Place Restaurant.

While it may be challenging to explore all three plantations in a single day, visiting two is certainly feasible.

To reach the Ashley River Plantations, depart from downtown Charleston and follow Highway 17 S to Highway 61 N, also recognized as Ashley River Road. Drayton Hall awaits just 12 miles from downtown, ready to immerse visitors in its rich history and breathtaking surroundings.

Stroll a swampy forest at Congaree National Park.

The Boardwalk Loop Trail at Congaree National Park meanders through the largest contiguous old-growth bottomland forest in the United States.

Here, you'll find yourself strolling amidst expanses of dark muck and a soggy woodland populated by bald cypress, tupelo, and hardwoods—an experience that's simultaneously eerie and mesmerizing. From mid-May through mid-June, visitors can witness the captivating sight of synchronous fireflies blinking in unison—a rare spectacle that occurs in only a handful of places worldwide. For those seeking aquatic adventures, the Cedar Creek Canoe Trail offers a fifteen-mile paddling path through the primeval forest.

To reach Congaree National Park, embark on a journey 105 miles northwest of Charleston via I-26 W, I-95 N, and a series of picturesque country highways.

Explore the Charleston County Sea Islands

Explore the Charleston County Sea Islands, where opportunities abound for paddling, learning, and soaking up the sun on the barrier islands nestled south of Charleston. On St. James Island, delve into the history of McLeod Plantation through insightful tours, shedding light on the lives of the plantation's former owners and the enslaved African Americans who resided and toiled here.

Witness the ageless majesty of the centuries-old Angel Oak Tree on Johns Island, one of the oldest living organisms east of the Mississippi River. Just a stone's throw away, Kiawah Beachwalker Park beckons with its pristine sands—the sole publicly accessible beach on the upscale Kiawah Island.

Rent a bike to traverse the ten miles of scenic shoreline or embark on a kayaking tour to explore the island's coastal marshes. For history enthusiasts, a visit to Wadmalaw Island unveils the Charleston Tea Garden, the sole tea plantation in the country.

To access the Charleston County Sea Islands, set out from Charleston and follow U.S. 17 S to Folly Rd Blvd. Turn left and continue until you reach Country Club Dr, leading to McLeod Plantation. Follow SC-700 W to reach the Angel Tree and the tea garden, and veer left at S.R. 10-20 from SC-700 W to arrive at Kiawah.

Unwind at Brookgreen Gardens

Nestled amidst former rice plantations, Brookgreen Gardens beckons with its captivating blend of botanical wonders and artistic treasures. Spanning over 9,000 acres, these sprawling gardens boast the largest collection of American figurative statuary in the United States, creating a tranquil haven where nature and art harmonize seamlessly. Anchored by an alley of majestic live oaks dating back 250 years, the gardens exude a sense of grandeur and serenity.

Don't miss the enchanting Night of 1000 Candles, when the grounds come alive with the flickering glow of candles and lights, casting a magical spell over the surroundings. For those seeking culinary delights, the Rustic Table in nearby Pawleys Island offers delectable Southern comfort food to satisfy any palate.

To embark on this enchanting journey, venture 80 miles north of Charleston via U.S. 17N to reach Murrells Inlet, where Brookgreen Gardens awaits.

Myrtle Beach is a mere 16 miles north of this verdant oasis, providing ample opportunity for further exploration and relaxation.

Discover the vibrant pulse of Columbia.

The dynamic state capital and home of the University of South Carolina. The revitalized Main Street District buzzes with a plethora of new dining establishments, whimsical public art installations, and the internationally acclaimed Columbia Museum of Art. Be sure to visit the beloved Nickelodeon arthouse theater for a cinematic experience like no other. Dive into the vibrant atmosphere of the Soda City

Market, spanning a four-block stretch of Main Street on Saturday mornings.

At the renowned Riverbanks Zoo & Gardens, ranked among America's top zoos, marvel at majestic lions, graceful giraffes, and playful penguins before embarking on an exhilarating ziplining adventure over the Saluda River. Quench your thirst with craft beer at the Hunter-Gatherer Brewery at the Hangar, or indulge in Cajun-Creole fare and fine whiskey at Bourbon.

Don't forget to embark on the city's Pimento Cheese Passport, guiding you to 14 must-visit destinations for sampling this beloved Southern delicacy.

To reach Columbia, follow I-26 west to exit 115, then continue on US 321 N until you reach the vibrant heart of the city, located 115 miles from Charleston.

Chapter 8: Beyond 2025: Future Travel Trends in South Carolina

Sustainable Tourism Initiatives in South Carolina

South Carolina, known for its breathtaking landscapes, rich history, and vibrant culture, has taken significant strides toward promoting sustainable tourism initiatives. With a focus on preserving its natural beauty and cultural heritage, the state has implemented various measures to ensure that visitors can explore its wonders while minimizing their impact on the environment.

One of the key sustainable tourism initiatives in South Carolina is the promotion of eco-friendly accommodations. From eco-lodges nestled in the heart of lush forests to solar-powered hotels along the coastline, travelers have a wide range of sustainable lodging options to choose from. These establishments prioritize energy efficiency, waste reduction, and water conservation, allowing tourists to enjoy their stay while minimizing their carbon footprint.

To encourage responsible travel, South Carolina has also developed a comprehensive transportation system that promotes sustainable mobility. Visitors can take advantage of the state's extensive network of bike paths and pedestrian-friendly streets, making it easy to explore cities and towns on foot or by bike. Additionally, the state has invested in electric vehicle charging stations, making it convenient for eco-conscious travelers to explore the state in their electric cars.

South Carolina's commitment to sustainable tourism is further exemplified by its emphasis on protecting its natural resources. The state has established numerous protected areas, such as national parks, wildlife refuges, and nature reserves. These protected areas not only provide a haven for diverse flora and fauna but also offer visitors a chance to immerse themselves in nature through guided eco-tours and educational programs.

Moreover, South Carolina actively promotes responsible wildlife viewing and preservation. Travelers can participate in turtle conservation initiatives, where they can witness the nesting and hatching of endangered sea turtles. Additionally, bird-watching enthusiasts can explore the state's many bird sanctuaries, contributing to ongoing research and conservation efforts.

In line with its sustainable tourism initiatives, South Carolina has also embraced local and organic food practices. The state's farm-to-table movement ensures that visitors can savor fresh and locally sourced ingredients, supporting local farmers and reducing the carbon footprint associated with long-distance food transportation.

By implementing these sustainable tourism initiatives, South Carolina aims to create a harmonious balance between tourism and the conservation of its natural and cultural heritage. As a tourist, adventurer, traveler, or explorer, you have the opportunity to experience the wonders of South

Carolina while contributing to its sustainable future. Whether you choose to explore the pristine beaches, hike through majestic mountains, or immerse yourself in vibrant city life, your journey will be an adventure that respects and preserves the beauty of South Carolina for generations to come.

Emerging Destinations and Attractions

In the ever-changing landscape of travel, there is always a sense of excitement in discovering new destinations and attractions that have yet to be fully explored. South Carolina, with its rich history, diverse landscapes, and vibrant culture, is no exception. This subchapter aims to highlight the emerging destinations and attractions that are set to captivate the adventurous souls who seek to explore the wonders of the Palmetto State.

As the year 2024 approaches, South Carolina is undergoing a transformation, with several hidden gems emerging as must-visit destinations. From the majestic Blue Ridge Mountains to the picturesque coastline, there is an abundance of new attractions awaiting discovery.

In the Upstate region, adventurers will find themselves drawn to the vibrant city of Greenville. With its thriving art scene, charming downtown area, and proximity to the mountains, Greenville offers a unique blend of outdoor adventure and cultural experiences. Take a leisurely stroll along the Swamp Rabbit Trail, a scenic pathway that winds its way through parks, waterfalls, and downtown Greenville. For the more adventurous, hiking through the nearby Pisgah National Forest or exploring the stunning beauty of Table Rock State Park will leave you in awe.

Moving towards the coast, the charming town of Beaufort is garnering attention as an emerging destination. Known for its antebellum architecture, historic sites, and pristine beaches, Beaufort offers a glimpse into the rich Southern heritage of South Carolina. Take a guided tour through the historic district, visit the stunning Hunting Island State Park, or embark on a kayak adventure through the salt marshes, where you can spot unique wildlife and immerse yourself in the tranquility of nature.

For those seeking a taste of the Lowcountry, the town of Bluffton beckons with its unique blend of Old South charm and contemporary flair. From exploring the vibrant arts and culture scene to indulging in delectable cuisine at local farm-to-table restaurants, Bluffton offers a delightful escape for the discerning traveler. Embark on a scenic boat tour along the May River, where you can spot dolphins playing in the wake or try your hand at fishing in the abundant waters.

As South Carolina continues to evolve as a premier travel destination, these emerging destinations and attractions provide a glimpse into the future of adventure travel in the Palmetto State. Whether you are a nature lover, a history buff, or simply seeking an off-the-beaten-path experience, South Carolina promises to offer something extraordinary. So, pack your bags, grab your sense of adventure, and embark on a journey through the lesser-known corners of this captivating state. The ultimate adventure awaits in South Carolina in 2024 and beyond.

Technological Advancements in Travel Planning

In this fast-paced digital era, technological advancements have revolutionized the way we plan our travel adventures. South Carolina, with its vast landscapes, rich history, and vibrant culture, is no exception. The state has embraced these advancements to enhance the travel planning experience for tourists, adventurers, travelers, and explorers.

One of the most remarkable technological advancements in travel planning is the rise of immersive virtual reality (VR) experiences. Nowadays, you can virtually explore South Carolina's breathtaking natural wonders, historic landmarks, and vibrant cities from the comfort of your own home. These VR experiences provide an opportunity to get a sneak peek into what awaits you in the Palmetto State, allowing you to plan your itinerary with more confidence and excitement.

Furthermore, mobile applications have become indispensable tools for travelers. With the touch of a button, you can access a wide range of travel apps that provide real-time information on attractions, accommodations, dining options, and transportation services. These apps enable you to plan your South Carolina adventure on the go, ensuring that you make the most of your time in the state.

Another noteworthy advancement is the integration of artificial intelligence (AI) in travel planning. AI-powered chatbots and virtual assistants can now help you with personalized recommendations, itinerary suggestions, and even language translation services. These AI companions ensure that you have a seamless and stress-free travel experience, allowing you to focus on exploring the wonders of South Carolina.

Additionally, the utilization of big data has transformed the way we make travel decisions. Travel websites and platforms now analyze vast amounts of data to offer personalized recommendations tailored to your preferences. Whether you are seeking outdoor adventures, cultural experiences, or culinary delights, these platforms can curate a travel itinerary that perfectly suits your interests.

South Carolina's travel industry has also incorporated advancements in sustainability and eco-friendly practices. Online platforms now allow travelers to choose accommodation options that prioritize environmental conservation and support local communities. This way, you can contribute to the preservation of South Carolina's natural beauty while enjoying a truly immersive and responsible travel experience.

In conclusion, technological advancements have revolutionized the way we plan our travel adventures in

South Carolina. Through virtual reality, mobile applications, artificial intelligence, and big data analysis, tourists, adventurers, travelers, and explorers can now plan their itineraries with greater ease, efficiency, and personalization. Embrace these advancements and embark on an unforgettable journey through South Carolina's captivating landscapes, rich history, and vibrant culture.

Cultural Exchange Programs and Volunteer Opportunities

In the vibrant state of South Carolina, there is so much more to explore than just its breathtaking landscapes and historic landmarks. For tourists, adventurers, travelers, and explorers seeking a deeper connection with the local community, engaging in cultural exchange programs and volunteer opportunities can be an enriching experience. These activities not only allow you to immerse yourself in the state's diverse cultural tapestry but also provide an opportunity to give back to the communities that make South Carolina so unique.

South Carolina is home to a rich blend of cultures, ranging from the Gullah Geechee people, who have preserved their

African heritage through language, arts, and traditions, to Native American tribes like the Catawba Nation. By participating in cultural exchange programs, you can engage with these communities, learn about their history, and develop a greater appreciation for their contributions to the state's cultural mosaic.

Numerous organizations offer cultural exchange programs that allow you to live with local families, learn their customs and traditions, and even participate in traditional activities such as basket weaving, storytelling, or cooking regional delicacies. These programs create lasting connections, fostering mutual understanding between visitors and locals.

For those looking to make a positive impact during their travels, South Carolina also offers a wide array of volunteer opportunities. From environmental conservation projects to community development initiatives, you can lend a helping hand and contribute to the well-being of the state's communities.

Engaging in volunteer work can involve activities like beach cleanups, habitat restoration, or assisting in local schools or community centers. These opportunities not only allow you to give back but also provide a unique chance to interact with locals and gain a deeper understanding of their daily lives.

While exploring South Carolina, consider dedicating a portion of your trip to a cultural exchange program or volunteer opportunity. Not only will you create unforgettable memories, but you will also leave a positive impact on the communities you encounter. By fostering cross-cultural understanding and supporting local initiatives, you become an active participant in preserving the diversity and heritage of South Carolina.

Remember, South Carolina is not just a destination; it's an invitation to connect, learn, and contribute to the tapestry of cultures that make this state a true adventure for the curious traveler.

Tips for Responsible Travel in South Carolina

As travelers, adventurers, and explorers, it is our responsibility to travel in a way that respects and preserves the natural beauty and cultural heritage of the places we visit. South Carolina, with its stunning landscapes, vibrant history, and welcoming communities, offers a wealth of opportunities for responsible travel. By following a few simple tips, we can ensure that our visit to the Palmetto State leaves a positive impact on its environment and communities.

1. Respect the Environment: South Carolina is blessed with diverse ecosystems, from pristine beaches to lush forests. Take care to leave no trace when visiting these natural wonders. Pack out your trash, stay on designated trails, and avoid disturbing wildlife. By leaving the environment as you found it, you help preserve it for future generations of travelers to enjoy.

2. Support Local Businesses: South Carolina is home to a vibrant community of artisans, farmers, and small business owners. Make an effort to support these local businesses by choosing locally-owned accommodations, dining in family-owned restaurants, and purchasing souvenirs from local artisans. By doing so, you contribute to the local economy and help sustain the unique character of the state.

3. Learn and Respect the Culture: South Carolina has a rich cultural heritage deeply rooted in its history and traditions. Take the time to learn about the local customs and respect them during your visit. Engage with the local communities, visit historical sites, and attend cultural events to gain a deeper understanding of the state's unique identity. By showing respect for the local culture, you enrich your own travel experience and foster mutual understanding.

4. Conserve Resources: South Carolina is known for its warm climate and abundant water sources. Be mindful of your water usage, particularly during times of drought, and conserve energy by turning off lights and electronics when not in use. Consider using public transportation or renting bicycles to explore the cities, reducing your carbon footprint and supporting sustainable travel options.

5. Give Back: Finally, consider giving back to the community you visit. Volunteer your time with local organizations, participate in beach cleanups, or support conservation efforts. By actively contributing to the well-being of the places you visit, you become a steward for responsible travel and leave a lasting positive impact.

By following these tips for responsible travel in South Carolina, you can ensure that your adventure in the Palmetto State is not only thrilling but also sustainable and respectful. Let's explore this beautiful state while leaving behind only memories and footprints, preserving its natural wonders, and supporting its vibrant communities for future generations to enjoy.

Recommended Books and Websites for Further Exploration

As you embark on your thrilling adventure in South Carolina, it's essential to equip yourself with the right resources to make the most of your journey. Whether you are a tourist, adventurer, traveler, or explorer, this subchapter presents a curated list of books and websites that will enhance your experience in the beautiful state of South Carolina.

Books:

1. **"Moon South Carolina" by Jim Morekis:** This comprehensive travel guide provides insider tips, detailed maps, and itineraries to help you navigate the state like a local. Discover hidden gems, historic landmarks, and outdoor adventures to create unforgettable memories.

2. **"Charleston: A Historic Walking Tour" by Robert N. Rosen:** Immerse yourself in the history and charm of Charleston, one of South Carolina's most iconic cities. This guide takes you on a captivating journey through the cobblestone streets, showcasing the city's rich heritage and architectural wonders.

3. "The Beaches of South Carolina" by Liz Mitchell: Dive into the coastal beauty of South Carolina with this book that highlights the state's stunning beaches. From Hilton Head to Myrtle Beach, explore the sandy shores, vibrant communities, and recreational activities available along the coastline.

Websites:

1. DiscoverSouthCarolina.com: The official website of South Carolina's tourism department offers a wealth of information on attractions, events, accommodations, and outdoor activities. Plan your itinerary, get insider tips, and stay updated on the latest happenings across the state.

2. SouthCarolinaParks.com: If you're a nature enthusiast or outdoor adventurer, this website is a must-visit. It provides details on the state parks, hiking trails, camping sites, and recreational opportunities available in South Carolina. Get ready to explore the diverse landscapes and immerse yourself in the beauty of nature.

3. HistoricCharleston.org: For history buffs, this website is a treasure trove of information about Charleston's rich past. Discover historic sites, museums, and walking tours that will transport you to a bygone era. Learn about the city's pivotal role in American history and explore its architectural gems.

By utilizing these recommended books and websites, you will be well-equipped to delve into the wonders of South Carolina. Whether you're seeking thrilling adventures, cultural experiences, or tranquil moments in nature, these resources will serve as your compass, ensuring you make the most of your journey in the Palmetto State. Happy exploring!

Useful Contacts and Emergency Numbers

When embarking on an adventure in South Carolina, it is crucial to have access to important contacts and emergency numbers to ensure a safe and enjoyable trip. Whether you are a tourist, adventurer, traveler, or explorer, this section provides you with essential information to navigate the beautiful landscapes and vibrant cities of South Carolina.

Emergency Numbers:

In case of any emergencies during your stay in South Carolina, it is important to know the following emergency numbers:

1. Police/Fire/Ambulance: 911

This is the general emergency number that connects you to the appropriate services in case of any immediate danger or threat.

2. South Carolina Highway Patrol:

If you encounter any road-related issues or require assistance during your journey, contact the South Carolina Highway Patrol at 711

3. Coastal Resource Enforcement:

For any emergencies related to the coastal areas, including wildlife incidents or environmental concerns, contact the Coastal Resource Enforcement at [Tel: (843) 953-0200].

Useful Contacts:

Apart from emergency services, having access to other important contacts can greatly enhance your South Carolina adventure. Here are some useful contacts to have on hand:

1. Local Visitor Centers:

Each city and region in South Carolina has its own visitor centers that provide maps, brochures, and recommendations for local attractions and activities. Save the contact information of the visitor centers in the areas you plan to explore.

10. CHARLESTON VISITOR CENTER
- 375 Meeting Street
- (800) 774-0006

11. KIAWAH ISLAND VISITOR CENTER
- 4475 Betsy Kerrison Parkway
- (800) 774-0006

12. MOUNT PLEASANT VISITOR CENTER
- 99 Harry M. Hallman, Jr. Boulevard
- (800) 774-0006

13. NORTH CHARLESTON VISITOR CENTER
- 4975-B Centre Point Drive
- (800) 774-0006

2. Consulates/Embassies:

If you are a foreign traveler, it is advisable to keep the contact details of your home country's consulate or embassy in case of any legal or emergency situations.

3. Medical Facilities:

Research and note down the contact information of nearby hospitals, clinics, and pharmacies in the areas you plan to visit. This ensures you have access to medical assistance if needed.

Remember to store these numbers in your phone, write them down in a travel journal, or keep them in a safe place for easy access. By being prepared with these useful contacts and emergency numbers, you can confidently embark on your South Carolina adventure, knowing that help and support are just a phone call away.

Conclusion

As you reach the end of "South Carolina InsideOut: Your Ultimate Travel Guide 2024 & Beyond," we hope you've found inspiration, guidance, and excitement for your upcoming adventures in the Palmetto State. Throughout this journey, we've strived to provide you with the tools and knowledge necessary to make the most of your time in South Carolina.

From uncovering the rich history of this storied land to indulging in its culinary delights, from exploring its breathtaking natural wonders to immersing yourself in its vibrant culture, South Carolina offers a wealth of experiences waiting to be discovered. We've equipped you with insider tips, detailed maps, and essential information to ensure that your exploration of this beautiful state is as seamless and enjoyable as possible.

But our journey doesn't end here. "South Carolina InsideOut" is not just a guidebook; it's a doorway to endless possibilities and adventures. As you venture forth, remember to embrace the unknown, savor every moment, and open yourself to new experiences.

Whether you're traversing the cobblestone streets of Charleston, basking in the natural splendor of the Blue Ridge Mountains, or savoring the flavors of Lowcountry cuisine, let the spirit of South Carolina guide you.

We invite you to keep this guide close at hand as you embark on your South Carolina journey, allowing it to serve as your trusted companion and source of inspiration. And as you explore the wonders of the Palmetto State, may you create memories that will last a lifetime.

Thank you for choosing "South Carolina InsideOut" as your travel companion. Here's to new beginnings, unforgettable adventures, and the magic of discovery. Have a safe trip, and may your South Carolina journey be filled with joy, wonder, and endless exploration.

If you found "South Carolina InsideOut: Your Ultimate Travel Guide 2024 & Beyond" to be helpful and informative, we kindly invite you to leave a review on Amazon.

Your feedback is invaluable and greatly appreciated as it helps other travelers discover the wonders of South Carolina and find their own memorable experiences.

Thank you for considering sharing your thoughts with fellow adventurers. Safe travels!

Made in the USA
Monee, IL
18 December 2024

74216272R10085